The Art of Wooden Bc

The Art of Wooden Boat Repair
How to Save Wood Boats

by
Allen Cody Taube

SeaStory Press

NOTE FROM THE AUTHOR

This book is not about repairs to lapstrake construction, plywood dinghies, model boats, or ships in a bottle, but concerns major structural repairs to the most popular and traditional construction method of large carvel, plank-on-frame wooden boats.

The Art of Wooden Boat Repair, How to Save Wood Boats

Third Edition; Copyright © 2018 by Allen Cody Taube

Cover Concept and Design: Cody Taube and Jessie Czopek

Illustrations by Allen Cody Taube

Rendering Assistance by Michele Taube

This book is the new, updated revision of *The Art of Wooden Boat Repair, A Boatwright's Secret Tricks of the Trade,* published in 2013 by Granny Apple Publishing of Sarasota FL.

The original version was titled *The Boatwright's Companion,* Copyright 1986 by Allen Taube and published in 1986 by International Marine Publishing Company, Camden, Maine.

Library of Congress Control Number: 2018956777

ISBN 978-1-936818-48-8

SeaStory Press
1508 Seminary St., Ste. 2
Key West FL 33040

PRINTED IN THE UNITED STATES OF AMERICA

A Note From the Publisher of This Edition

The Art of Wooden Boat Repair has enjoyed continuous popularity since it was first released in 1986. In this edition Capt. Allen Cody Taube includes many updates and additions. I am honored to be the new publisher of this valuable resource.

The carvel plank style of boatbuilding dates to the ocean-going ships built in Iberia during the great Age of Discovery (ca. 14th-15th centuries AD). Clearly some techniques and principles remain unchanged. But tools and available materials do change, and so ongoing updates are in order.

Also, I have made some formatting changes to make the book easier to use. Font size and line spacing are increased to make the text easier to read, especially when laying open on the workbench of a person with tools in hand. I have also expanded and updated the Table of Contents and Index to make it easier to find specific information.

Coincidently, I first met Capt. Al in '86 when I sailed with my family into Safe Harbor Marina in the Florida Keys, aboard a 43 foot Kettenburg mahogany sloop, built in the '60s in San Diego. We brought her down the Pacific coast and through the Panama Canal on a 7-month trip that remains one of my fondest memories. So I say, along with Capt. Al:

"Long Live Wooden Boats!"

Sheri Lohr, publisher SeaStory Press

A Note from the Publisher of the Second Edition

When I read Allen's first (now out of print) book about repairing wooden boats, *The Boatwright's Companion,* written in 1986, I knew, as an admirer of beautiful wooden boats, how important it would be to put this book back into print. I saw that it contained valuable information that needed to be preserved and passed on. It was what I call "written with love," written with a passion, care, dedication and sincerity that is scarcely found in books of this type today.

It would have been easier to put his first book back into print the way it was, but Allen insisted that he have a chance to re-write the book with the insight and hindsight that comes with the 28 years since he wrote the first edition.

When I read his new manuscript, I could tell right away that this book was the real thing and I knew that it had to be available for any and all wooden boat owners and wooden boat lovers to read in the interest of keeping wooden boats alive. This is why I decided that Granny Apple Publishing must publish this book.

I feel very good and proud of this decision and I know you will cherish and appreciate *The Art of Wooden Boat Repair.* Boat Repair is, as you will see, very much an art.

Janet Verdeguer, Granny Apple Publishing

PRAISE FROM A FELLOW BOATWRIGHT

Twenty-eight years ago I had the opportunity to read Al Taube's first book about boat repair. I was a cabinetmaker who loved old wooden boats and decided to steer my career in that direction. The simple straightforward, no nonsense approach to boat repair that Al taught sent me in the right direction. Later, I had the opportunity to work with Al on his own boat at which time he taught me his invaluable method for making templates, a pre-requisite for wooden boat repair.

Though there are many lessons to be learned in *The Art of Wooden Boat Repair*, the lessons on template making are applicable to even the most experienced. As a boatwright who has owned his own business for the past 27 years, that simple lesson has allowed me to do very compound curves in the process of building bulkheads to installing new planks and constructing complicated built-in furniture and in the most pragmatic way has been worth about an extra $20 per hour!

Thank you Al Taube.

Jimmy Wray, Key West

February 4, 2014

TABLE OF CONTENTS

INTRODUCTION TO WOOD BOATS

It all started for me many years ago on a boat delivery from Medemblik on the northeast coast of Holland to Hawaii. I was one of a crew of three on a large wooden doomed Baltic Trader sailboat - we were short-handed, smashing through treacherous November gales in the cold and dangerous North Sea. The boat was leaking bad. It was coming apart. We tried to tuck into port, but we flew a German flag and were not welcome in Holland. We limped into Amsterdam and motored through the Nord Sea Canal to Rotterdam afloat on our bilge pumps. More gales were headed our way. Worse than before. Shortly after we got off the boat, it went down with all hands in the North Sea. It was then that I vowed to learn how to fix wood boats.

After that near-fatal experience I took a two-year wooden boat-building apprenticeship in Mill Valley California and learned how to build and repair wood boats. Later a few friends from the class formed a boat-building co-op on what remained of an old shipyard on the historic waterfront of the "Gates" of Sausalito, California.

It was a dying art, and we were all struggling to become the next generation of noble wood boat saviors. The old shipwrights who still lived there would come by to watch us work. They appreciated our energy and dedication but would shake their heads and frown when we were doing wrong, smile and nod when we were doing right. They were old and dying and a few of them were generous enough to pass on to us the tricks of the trade that they had spent a lifetime hoarding.

None of us young guys dared call ourselves "shipwrights." That was a word of respect we reserved for the senior generation. We called ourselves "wood butchers."

I learned to plank with a spiling batten and a pair of dividers the old way. The shipwright who taught me had lots of experience. I followed his procedure without ever a doubt. The books and magazine articles that I had read on the subject all confirmed his method (and still do). After putting in a few easy planks on small boats, I soon felt like a full-fledged professional planker.

One day, I was as a planker on a large wooden boat, the *Raven*. We were two of us plankers, Rick Cogswell and I. Peter Lamb cut out new frames on a big band saw and caulked. Scott Diamond chopped out the rotten planks and frames with a chainsaw. We had contracted to replace a quarter of the bottom planking and framing in ten days. The boat had 2-inch-thick fir planks. On the morning of the first day, I made my spiling batten (planking template) and cut out the first eighteen-foot plank. Then I dragged it over to the boat and began to drive it in overhead using 4 x 4 shores and wedges.

The new plank was exactly the reverse, the mirror-image, the opposite of the planking space. Peter Lamb asked me what was wrong. I told him exactly what I had done. Then told me the secret, the missing step that almost everyone makes. (See chapter on planking). I tried it Peter's way and the plank fit! The template had been so accurate that the plank just about fell in and fit perfectly. Thank you, Peter Lamb.

When you build a new boat, you steam the planks and bend them up or down or *edge-set* them, forcing them to fit with clamps and wedges. When you repair a wood boat, and replace a single plank, you have to make a template so accurate that you turn a two-dimensional shape to fit a three-dimensional space <u>without</u> *edge-set.*

Even today I see new articles in magazines, videos on You-Tube, and books that, if followed, will produce planks that will be mirror-image or backwards and will <u>not</u> fit. Professional and well-known boat builders are intimidated by the "shutter plank" or "whiskey plank" (fitting the single plank). If this were true of planking templates, then it is also true of all templates whether for a bulkhead, a knee, a floor timber, anything… Say you've made a template to cut out a carpet, when you go to cut out the carpet, you turn the carpet over to the woven side because it would be hard to cut it out through the fuzzy pile side. If you place your template on the woven side, trace it and cut it out, you will find that the carpet won't fit the space at all.

How was it that all those books and magazine articles had omitted such an important step? I realized that somewhere along the line, something important had been lost. The more I thought about it, the more I realized that wooden boat repair was becoming a lost art. Something had to be done to record the correct information. These tricks of the trade needed to be passed on, not horded. There were fewer and fewer old-timers left. They had killed themselves off with arsenic, copper, mercury, lead, and other nice boat-building poisons and had neglected to pass on their secrets to the younger generations.

Unless the shipwright is willing to share his knowledge, the traditional wood boat is in very real danger of extinction.

Wood boats are becoming the dinosaurs of the technical age. Everyone wants fiberglass boats. Wood boats are too much maintenance, too much work. If nobody is left to care for them, then they too will die just as the great clipper ships did at the onslaught of the age of steel and steam.

So to the great wood ships of yesterday ... to the great wood boats of today… to the old-time shipwrights who had no one to leave their legacy ... to all the forests and to all the trees ... to all the dreamers and to all the dreams ... to all the wood sloops and schooners surfing on a broad reach, bound for a distant island ... to the wood trawlers, wood tugs and wood fishing boats ... the salty sea and the sail full of wind ... to the great seamen of history who sailed the winds of commerce in ships we may see no more ... and to you who care about wooden boats—because their future is in your hands—to all of you do I dedicate this book.

If nothing else is learned from this book besides *How to Make a Good Template* and *How to Work with a Good Attitude,* then my goal will be fulfilled. You will have the two most important tools necessary for success in any boat-building endeavor, and the wood boat, part history, part dream, made from the heart of the forest, will sail the seas forever.

WHY WOOD BOATS?

Getting a boat and sailing the sea is a dream for many. But not many can afford this luxurious dream. In this age of technology and need for instant gratification, wooden boats have become *almost* obsolete. They are associated with idealists, dreamers and a lot of work. However, the traditional designs of many wood boats can be traced back to ways that were proven by time and trial by sea. Many of the newer fiberglass boats, however, are designed to look good, have huge cockpits for happy-hour cocktails, large beds and bedrooms, spacious clothes lockers, roomy heads and big modern galleys with marble countertops so that they will appeal to the wives and sell at the boat shows. As a result, a lot of them have huge, ungainly transoms to allow for that big spacious aft cabin bedroom and very pointy bows, so they can motor into a chop. At sea, in rough conditions, a good boat *must* have balanced ends. At sea, many of these modern boats make no sense.

Nothing moves through the water like a good wood boat. Every square inch of it wants to float, to lift, to surf, to dance on top of the sea. Not fiberglass, not steel, not cement, not aluminum—nothing has the grace of a good wood boat. A wood boat has life. A wood boat is alive.

Legendary waterman and tugboat captain Lane Briggs from Rebel Marine in Norfolk, Virginia once said: "a wood boat has life and can reach deep into itself and pull out more than she is physically capable of." I have witnessed that while surfing down huge waves in a Pacific tsunami with a rooster-tail coming off the stern of my wood schooner. Looking up at the next wave and wondering how my little double-ended schooner could possibly rise to it, but she did with style and grace, never once tripping or broaching on the crest of those monsters. A wood boat has soul, spirit, life. Maybe it comes from the life of the forest, the life of the trees cut down to make her; maybe it comes from the hands and hearts of those who built her. If you have made the commitment to own a wooden boat you might find out what Lane means.

Wood is one of the strongest materials by weight.

Strength of material per-weight is one of the most important boatbuilding considerations.

The three classic measurements of material strength are: Tension (bending resistance), Torsion (twisting resistance) and Compression (squashing) resistance.

If you think steel is stronger than wood by weight you may be wrong. Here's proof: take a one-foot long common fir, Home Depot 2 x 4 and try to bend it, you will find it is incredibly resistant to bending. Try twisting it, you'll find it is almost impossible to twist. Then try compressing it with a hydraulic press. Wood is very strong because of all those long inter-locking tubes glued together with natural lignum glue.

Now try the same three tests on a sheet of steel weighing the same. The steel will easily bend. You can twist it. And yes, if you compress the steel it will distort.

Why else wood boats? Wood boats are built so they can be repaired.

If you are not afraid to work hard to rebuild that dream, by repairing and maintaining a wood boat, you can turn that dream into a reality. If you work and maintain your wood boat with integrity and make the right choices, you could end up with a great sea boat.

But first you must ask yourself if you are willing to invest your time, energy and money in repairing and constantly maintaining a wood boat? Are you willing to bucket-off the deck with saltwater after it rains? Haul it out every year to bottom- paint? Are you willing to keep the deck waterproof and repair rot, corrosion and deterioration? No boat is maintenance free, but are you willing to maintain a wood boat?

Be realistic and honest with yourself. If you do not have the time, money, tools and skills to repair or restore this boat, walk away and allow someone else to take it over.

One more thing: when considering buying or repairing that wood boat, ***never underestimate the power of the sea.***

SUSTAINABILITY

My son, Cody, a landscape architect and spokesman for the new generation, is concerned for this planet's survival. He says when we repair wood boats we need to think of renewable resources. We need to stop wasting what is left Earth's old growth trees. We need to think about the rain forests biomass and forests all over the world where big corporations are clear-cutting, destroying natural wilderness, destroying rare plants and homes of endangered birds, animals, and indigenous tribes.

He is absolutely right. Repairing wood boats is by nature a renewable, sustainable effort. Instead of throwing away an old boat, and building a new one, fix it, save it, re-use it, sail it again. For many people with time but limited funds, the only way they can afford a boat is to get a wood boat and restore/repair it. Wood boats are designed to be repaired. When you first get your boat, and begin to make repairs, consider using recycled wood: wood from old buildings being torn down, recycled teak decking, and used boat gear. Pull wood out of construction dumpsters. They're usually stuffed full of perfectly good 2 x 4s, 2 x 6s and plywood. Don't forget to use bedding and seal all end-grain.

If you need to make a big hanging knee, lodging knee, or a gaff jaw, make a template and take it into the woods, or to a beach. Look for a standing dead tree, or a fallen tree, or driftwood that might contain the correct shape or curve, instead of going to the lumber yard and buying a new a ten-foot 3-inch x

18-inch white oak plank to cut the shape from. Besides being expensive, big old growth white oak trees are not renewable. They will eventually disappear and never come back.

Bamboo is the world's fastest growing and most renewable plant. Black locust– an exotic evasive species is considered a pest or weed it grows so fast and displaces indigenous plants—also Australian Pine is a great wood for boat building and is a common driftwood all through the southern states. Use Ipe instead of teak; bio resins instead of petroleum resins; a mixture of beeswax and corn oil, or cedar oil instead of petroleum-based preservatives. Tidewater cypress is great boatbuilding wood, shipworms won't eat it, nor will termites, and it is very rot resistant. Use Trex (recycled plastic and sawdust formed into planks used for home outdoor decking) for rub rails and wormshoes.

Find cleats and blocks and fittings at yard sales, used boat gear stores, old derelict boats at boat yards. No need to buy a brand new cleat or porthole for a fifty- year-old boat you are restoring.

If part of a timber has some rot, replace that part, if you can make the repair without compromising the structure of that timber. It is usually not necessary to replace an entire good timber if only a small part of it is rotten.

As a way of saying thank you for the trees used to build or rebuild your wood boat, plant trees for the next generation.

1
DEVELOPING A GOOD WORKING ATTITUDE

Building and repair are slow magic. The process is a stubborn, brutal, physical, and passionate battle. It was once said that "success is constancy of purpose." Approaching your work with a good attitude is the first step toward success. The second is organization. The third is making a good template. With a good attitude, organization, constancy of purpose, and an accurate template, success is inevitable.

Using your body and its energy to do work

How to work is one of the most important lessons we can learn as we grow older. When we are young we have tremendous energy, but have not yet learned how to use these energies. We must learn how to position ourselves in such a way as to best focus our energy on our work.

Avoid abusing your natural energies, such as gritting your teeth, tightening your jaw, or tensing your stomach, leg or back muscles while you are working. Consciously try to relax—focus your energy only on that part of your body that is doing the work. This will give you greater endurance and control. When your energy is low, do not continue to work. Resume working only when your energy and inspiration returns.

Physical comfort

Physical comfort is very important in working efficiently and keeping a good attitude. If you are working outside, shade yourself from the sun. If you are working below, or in a poorly ventilated area, especially at all times when working with chemicals, have a fan nearby to bring fresh air. Wear knee pads or use a cushion when kneeling as well as one for your head if you must lie down to work. Use a bench, milk crate or stool to sit on.

Leather gloves will protect your hands when working with metal, or when surgically removing material with a sledge hammer and a wrecking bar. Always wear plastic or rubber gloves when mixing or using epoxies, resins, and paints.

Wear a dust mask and safety goggles when grinding or sanding. Wear a disposable paper suit when grinding or painting toxic bottom paint. Protect your eyes and ears. Use a good clean respirator around all toxins.

Optimism

Be ever optimistic that you will succeed. Don't curse or swear or pity yourself when confronted by setbacks; instead, turn them into challenges.

Planning

Think out carefully the considerations and procedures from start to finish and organize the job before you begin.

Investigate and improve

Investigate the cause of the problem and correct it before fixing the damage it caused. Always aim at making it better than it was originally.

Work and life

Allow your work to become a part of your life, not just a job to do or to get over with. The choice to enjoy yourself while you work is yours. It is a rewarding decision.

Repairing you boat is just one part of the great journey. If you do good, honest, conscientious work, and you are lucky, your boat may reward you with a journey of a lifetime to faraway and wondrous places.

The sign in the captain's quarters of the square-rigged clipper ship Star of India says: *"Do Right, Fear Not."*

Don't try to hide or cover up problems

Remove rot and replace damaged wood with good wood. Never use "Bondo" on a wooden boat, it will make the rot worse. *Fix wood with wood.* Use epoxy for glue. Using products like "Git Rot" and other injected additives is only fooling yourself, they will never replace the long inter-locking grain structure of wood.

Sometimes you have to make a temporary repair when time,

materials or money are not available, to stop a deck leak and prevent fresh water from entering below or for other reasons. Don't forget that was only a temporary fix. Don't ever compromise the integrity of your boat.

Beware of free advice

Respect

Be humbled by the power of nature. Respect the sea, the wind, the weather. Respect and take good care of your wooden boat and sail her gently. Racing your wooden boat for glory and ego is hard on an old wooden boat and sometimes damaging and disrespectful. I have watched too many sailors break their boats trying to win a race.

Inspiration

Whatever the source of your inspiration, you must hold that inspiration with you as you work. Whether it be the inspiration from a loved one, from an object of natural beauty, from a reverence for wood, inspirational music, or from an inspirational dream. A good shower or a cup of strong coffee can be inspirational at the beginning of a long day or before attempting a difficult job that requires great concentration.

Inspiration adds passion and magic to your work, is reflected in the work it creates, and that work becomes an inspiration to others.

2
TOOLS

Use the right tool for the job, and if you don't have it, go out and buy it if you can. Chances are, you'll need it over and over again. Borrow tools only as a last resort—if you break it, you'll have to replace it, and you still won't have the tool you need next time. Check the swap meets or flea markets, the hand tools gotten there are usually much better than the modern–made in China–ones you can buy at the hardware store today.

Buy American-made tools whenever possible. Tools are meant to be used and, if necessary, used up—chisels especially. It's better to sharpen them often than not to use them for fear of getting them dull or wearing them out. Keep your chisels, knives and plane blades razor sharp at all times. Respect your tools. Store your planes on their sides.

Sharpening tools saves time. It will change your whole attitude. A sharp tool is like a sharp mind. Use a belt sander or bench grinder, either hand-operated or electric to "hollow grind" your blades. Then use the waterstones to sharpen the inside and outside edges leaving a curved valley between them. Hone the backside of the blade flat on the waterstone. Use the fine stone to polish the surfaces of the blade. (Figures 1 and 2)

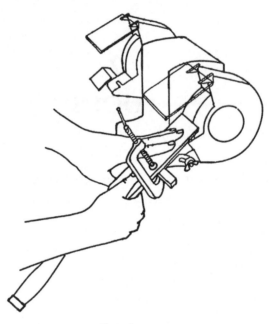

Figure 1

A chisel is hollow-ground on a bench grinder (or belt-sander's round end). To maintain the correct angle of attack, a small block of wood is C-clamped to the blade and held against the guide.

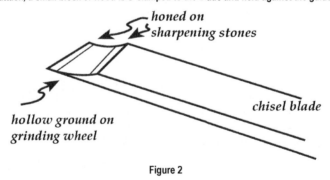

honed on sharpening stones

chisel blade

hollow ground on grinding wheel

Figure 2

Then use a leather strop or leather belt. When you get

done, the blade will be so sharp that with a light pass, you can shave the hair off your arm; and so shiny that you can see your smile in its mirror. Sharpening tools is a very important time. It gives you a chance to plan your work before you start, and gives you a nice break when you need to sharpen your energy as well; it helps center and ground your energy. If you do not have a bench grinder or sharpening stones, at least use a good American-made, Nicholson mill bastard file to keep your tool blades sharp.

Wood-handled chisels should have steel rings or threaded plumbing pipes with caps to prevent them from splitting. Split handles on hammers can be fixed by wrapping them with tarred nylon and epoxy. In a pinch, a screwdriver or file can be sharpened to make a custom chisel. Be flexible and creative, make your own tools whenever you can. *Before you use your back, use your brain; your brain is stronger.*

Use shallow-angled wooden wedges to move things. Cut them out of a 2 x 4, 2 x 6, or 4 x 4 on a band saw or circular saw; make a stash of these before every job. Cut out a bunch of plywood pads for under C-clamps and behind wedges. Have a come-along handy and know how to tie rolling hitches, trucker's hitches, and Spanish windlasses.

HAND TOOLS

A house carpenter needs a hammer, a speed-square, a level, a circular saw, and a tape measure. A boat carpenter needs a truckload of tools. Here is a list of some of the essential hand tools needed to undertake a major boat repair job.

Screwdrivers—small, medium, large, Phillips, and slot

Center punch—*for* marking and starting drill holes in metal

Punches—for driving out bolts, drifts, and rivets. These can be made from rod or bolt.

Nail set

Spike set

Awl—for scribing cut-off marks and for gently probing into wood to determine whether it is sound

Sliding bevel gauge—for measuring angles or taking off bevels

Carpenter's square—a large, flat steel square, and a small square for marking 90° angles

Tape measure A 25-foot ¾-inch-wide steel tape is usually quite adequate (cloth tape measures stretch too much and won't give accurate readings). Use one that is marked clearly and is easy for you to read.

Speed square—for using as a guide when sawing 90 or 45-degree cuts

Long straight flexible battens—These are usually made out of fir or pine, are straight-grained, and should be held up to the eye and sighted for straightness or fairness. They can be cut out of scrap planking wood and stored flat to avoid warping.

Carpenter Pencils—Yellow is the best color for lead pencils, since red or blue ones blend in too well with the rest of the world and are easily lost. Carry a few spares in your tool box; it is inevitable that you will lose them. They should be kept sharp with a pocket knife, small block plane, or belt sander.

Sharp knife—for whittling plugs, stopwaters, sharpening lead pencils, checking seams for cotton, and checking wood (gently) for soft areas

Box of chalk—White or, even better, colored chalk is good for marking questionable areas when surveying the hull. It is also good for marking tight spots when fitting two pieces of wood together. And chalk is good for marking wet seams when the boat is first hauled.

Through-hull key—Made out of a flat ⅜ or ¼-inch piece of triangular-shaped steel plate. It fits into the through-hull from the outside and is used when tightening or removing a ball valve or sea cock.

Putty knife

Straight claw hammers—are more useful than curved claw hammers for boat work, because they can be hammered claw-first into a piece of wood by beating them on the head with another hammer. Hammers should have steel or fiberglass handles because they are often used for prying.

Short-handled sledge—a most useful tool

Ball peen hammer—for forming heads of drifts or rivets

Tapered drill bits—should be used when drilling for screws or iron boat nails (square nails). You should have the right ta-pered drill bit for each size screw that you use, especially for #10s, #12s, and #14s.

Figure 3
A spade bit for countersinking

Wood bore spade drill bits—for ¼, ⅜, ½, ⅝, ¾,⅞ and 1 inch. These are flat drill bits used for countersunk holes for fas-teners. (Although the type that fasten directly to the tapered drill bit with Allen-head set-screws for attaching counter-sinker have a nasty habit of expanding when they get hot from drilling and traveling up the drill bit, causing a deeper hole to be drilled for counter-sinking than is intended. If you must use this type, be careful). It is safer to use a spade bit (Figure 3) for counter-sinking.

High speed metal drill bits—from ¹⁄₁₆ to 1 inch. Because these bits grab and pull quickly into the wood, they are hard to stop at a specific depth and should not be used for drilling countersunk fastener holes in wood.

Assortment of augers—for ¼, ⅜, ½, ¾ and 1-inch screw augers, and barefoot augers for use with a hand-brace

Hand-brace—This is an excellent tool for drilling holes in wood and for driving and removing screws. You will have much more control on the amount of torque and will be able to feel how well the fastener is tightening by using a hand-brace- and-bit instead of an electric screwdriving device.

Screwdriving bits for hand-braces—come in small, medium, and large Phillips and slot. If you are unable to find the right-sized one to fit a particular screw head, a larger one or a bolt may be ground down on a bench grinder to fit the slot head of the screw.

Small hand block planes—usually between 5 and 6 inches long and can fit comfortably into one hand. They are by far the most popularly used hand plane and if you only have one plane, this is the size to have. Because block planes are shallow angle planes, they can also be used to plane end-grain. You may want a rabbet plane. The blade of this type of plane extends all the way to the edge of the sole. A plane with a rounded sole and blade is useful for hollowing the backsides of planks. Wooden-bodied planes are useful for planing wet wood. Specialized planes can be made out of a block of wood and their blades made from a section of a large band saw or hand saw blade, leaf spring or a file sharpened on a wheel to the correct angle and honed on a sharpening stone. Long-bodied planes are handy for fairing. Plane blades should be kept razor sharp. When sharpening them on a wheel, be careful not to overheat the metal. Dip the blade in water often to prevent burning them and losing the temper. When not being used, lay a plane on its side; this protects the blade from getting dull and rusty. Beeswax rubbed on the sole of the plane will help it slide smoothly.

Chisels—You should have one or two each ¼, ⅜, ½, ⅝, ¾

and 1-inch chisels and at least one large framing chisel or 'slick' about 2 inches or wider. If you can't afford to buy an expensive set, the common Fuller or Stanley, less expensive ones will do quite well if they are kept sharp. Just as an indication of how sharp is sharp, a new chisel is not sharp. It must be honed on sharpening stones so that its cutting edge and backside shine and so that it will shave the hair off the back of your hand with one light pass. Always move the chisel away from your fingers and other parts of your body. Specialized small chisels can be made by sharpening an old screwdriver, and larger ones by sharpening a file or rasp to the correct angle. Wear goggles when grinding metal. Protect the cutting edges of chisels when not in use by keeping them in a special slotted section of your toolbox, or in an oil-soaked canvas chisel envelope. Alternatively, a section of rubber hose can be cut and squeezed so that it fits tightly over the blade.

Hand saws—crosscut and rip. Again, beeswax rubbed along the blade make the saw cut more easily.

Hack saw—Carbide hacksaw blades are useful for sawing through bolts. Where there is no room for the saw and handle, some masking tape can be wrapped around the blade, and it can then be hand-held. Hacksaw blades are available for sawzalls and saber saws. Wear gloves, goggles, and use cutting oil when cutting through metal. A short section of a hacksaw blade can be used to clean out seams, between double frames, or between frame and plank. For cleaning out very narrow cracks the set of the teeth may be ground down. Two small pieces can be broken from the ends of a dull hacksaw blade and joined together with a rivet or small nut and bolt to form a very compact bevel gauge. (Figure 4)

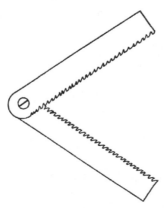

Figure 4
Small bevel gauge made out of a hacksaw blade

Backsaw and miterbox Coping saw or keyhole saw

Plastic spreader or squeegee—for spreading thickened epoxy glue or bedding compounds. Always spread glue and bedding on both surfaces to be joined together to avoid voids. Little V grooves can be cut in a plastic spreader if a thicker layer of bedding or glue is needed.

Rubber gloves—When painting or using epoxy or other harmful chemicals, always protect your skin from chemical absorption.

Leather gloves—When working with metal

Dust masks and respirators—whenever grinding or sanding wood, fiberglass or paint especially antifouling paint. Use cartridge respirator masks when working with chemical vapors. If

23

there are no masks available, a bandanna worn over your nose and mouth will help keep some of the dust out of your lungs. Mahogany and fir sawdust are probably the worst since they are very light and feathery and remain airborne for a long time. Old paint may contain lead, mercury, copper, arsenic. Take care of yourself; your boat will probably outlive you.

Scissors—for cutting cardboard templates

Metal file—for shaping metal, smoothing and sharpening edge tools

Wood rasp—for rough-shaping wood

Expansion bit for hand brace—for drilling large holes in wood

Hand-operated grinding wheels—are portable and clamp onto the work table. The wheel should turn smoothly and have an angle guide to rest the tool on when sharpening. This grinding wheel is used to hollow-grind the cutting edge.

Staple gun—for stapling form-fitting templates or joining spiling templates together

Fine and coarse sharpening stones—Japanese waterstones are made out of sandstone and are kept soaking in a bucket of water when not in use. The action is back and forth, without rocking the blade, keeping it flat and on a constant angle to the stone. The stones may be placed on a damp rag to prevent them from slipping.

The backside of the plane blade or chisel should be honed

flat on the stones and polished to a mirror shine. This will help them stay sharp longer. A guide can be used to keep the blade on the correct angle when sharpening the beveled edge. When the soft stone becomes ridged or bumpy, rub it wet on a cinderblock or rougher sharpening stone to resurface it. If you prefer to use oil-stones, that's okay. A good set of stones will last a lifetime.

Crow bar—for prying or pulling out nails or bolts

Flat pry bar

Small C-clamps—at least six small ones

Large C-clamps—at least six large C-clamps or bar clamps

Pipe clamps—at least three of these. They can be lengthened by using longer pipe threaded on one end.

Dividers—The type that have a way of locking the setting are the best for template making or spiling. The type with adjustable points are handy but not necessary. Those that can be used with a pencil must be stiff enough to keep a setting.

Caulking mallet—It is not essential to have one of these; a plastic, leather, or wooden mallet will do. Some prefer to use a hammer or small, short-handled sledge. Decent caulking mallets and caulking tools can still be found on Ebay or elsewhere on the internet. Use whatever you are comfortable with that allows you to have a feel for driving in the cotton.

Lead mallet—for driving galvanized fasteners. These will not chip the zinc coating.

Plastic mallet—used for surveying the hull to avoid denting the topside paint or bruising the wood fibers as a steel-headed hammer will.

Wood or leather mallet—for use with wooden-handled chisels. A steel ring can be cut from the end of a pipe and fitted over the wooden handle of a chisel to protect it from splitting.

Caulking irons—size 00, 0, and 1, a *Making (or dumb) Iron* for opening tight caulking seams or making them uniform before caulking, and a bent iron for caulking the garboard seam.

Caulking cotton—kept dry and clean in a caulking bag or bucket

Reefing iron—A traditional tool for reefing out seams. A horseshoe pick can be used for reefing or a reefing iron can be forged out of the tang of an old file or rasp.

Ratchet and socket wrench set—useful for tightening or loosening nuts or bolts *Crescent wrench, set of box-end wrenches, pipe wrenches.*

Vise Grips—can be used as C-clamps if necessary. When trying to pull a nail or bolt, a vise grip can be attached under the head and a pry bar used to pry against it. This method is especially useful when trying to remove headless nails.

Safety goggles—are very important when grinding or sanding metal, paint or wood. They should also be worn when sawing wood or metal with power tools.

Steel straightedge ruler

Chalk line

Vise—for holding metal while grinding bending, or shaping.

Table vise—like a "workmate" for holding objects while cutting drilling or planning.

Wood scrapers—1 and 2 inch.

Masking tape—for marking as a depth gauge on drill bits and to protect surfaces when gluing or painting.

Ball of string—when stretched between two nails, forms a straight reference line for measuring distances or curves, for taking off hull bevels when making frames, bulkheads, or floor timbers.

Length of rope—for making Spanish windlasses or trucker's hitches to secure, lift, or create tension.

Come-along—This is a wire spool ratchet winch that can be used to pull, lift, or move heavy objects.

Toothbrush and small paintbrush—for cleaning seams and brushing out the edges of planks and frames before replacing a plank

Wire brushes—A large wire brush can be used for cleaning sanding belts of belt sanders when the grit fills up. They can fit on a drill or grinder and be used to remove flaky paint and rust from iron keels and to clean rusty or corroded fittings. A small wire brush is useful for cleaning out through-hulls. A very small wire brush can be made by stripping back the plastic from one end of a short piece of plastic-coated rigging wire. These miniature wire brushes can be tightened in the chuck of an electric drill and used to brush the rust from the heads of rusty iron fasteners.

Propane torch—used for heating corroded fittings; when metal is heated it expands, and if two fittings are corroded together, heating the outside one will help to separate them. A propane torch can also be used to burn out a shipworm hole if it is not too deep or extensive. The hole is then filled with cement or epoxy putty. A special hood can be fitted over the canister for burning off paint. A propane torch can also be used for soldering copper sheathing or heating up nuts on bolts. Larger propane tanks can be used to fire up a steambox.

Chunk of beeswax—is used for rubbing on saw blades, table saw tables, and planes to help them slide and cut better. *Heat and melt beeswax (one part) and add corn oil (two to three parts) in a coffee can to make a waterproofing wood preservative to apply on wooden mast and bare wood surfaces.*

Hydraulic jack—can be used for seating wormshoes or when replacing deadwood. Timbers should be pressed firmly against each other with the aid of a jack to ensure tight joints before and during fastening. Hydraulic jacks can be used to drive or set drifts or remove keelbolts. A hydraulic jack may be needed to lift the boat when replacing a wormshoe or to remove a heavy rudder or keel.

Mirror and flashlight—are sometimes needed to locate keelbolts under the ballast keel or when checking for rot or broken frames behind stringers or ceilings.

Knee pads—to protect your knees when kneeling

Plug cutters—the type with four cutting blades makes the best wood plugs.

Caulking gun

Wooden wedges—shallow angled wedges for moving or lifting timbers or seating planks

Blocks of wood and pads—for under clamps.

Cheater pipe—length of steel or aluminum pipe that fits over the handle of a crescent wrench or pipe wrench for more leverage

ELECTRIC TOOLS

Electric reversible, variable speed drill—½-inch drill is best

Saber saw, Sawzall or reciprocal saw

Router—with a box of router bits; carbide bits are worth the extra money.

Electric bench grinder—If you are lucky enough to have one of these, be sure to get one that has a slow speed. A fast-turning wheel overheats the metal too quickly and then the temper is lost. You can tell you have got it too hot when the edge turns black or blue. Constantly dip the tool in water while it is being sharpened to cool it. It also helps to scribe a line across the back of the blade with a carpenter's awl or pencil to keep it square. A short wooden block can be C-clamped to the back of the blade and held firmly under the guide to insure that the blade is being sharpened straight and square. Always wear goggles or use an eye shield.

Belt sander—A most useful tool with a good supply of 24, 36, 50, 80, 100-grit belts. If the belt sander is flat on top, without protruding knobs or handles, it can be turned on its back, held in a vise, and used as a table sander.

Disc grinder—with a soft foam pad and assorted sanding discs. A slow or variable-speed grinder (that slows to 2000 RPMs or less) is best for use on wood. Higher speeds will burn paint or melt the glue around glued wood plugs. When using a soft pad grinder for fairing the hull, hold the pad flat against the surface and keep the grinder moving constantly. Never use a hard pad or hard disc on a wooden hull. Don't use the edge of the pad, it will gouge the wood.

Random orbital sander

Circular saw—with a sharp carbide combination blade, rip blade, and fine-tooth blade

Small portable table saw and band saw

Wood shop—The use of a wood shop that has a thickness planer, band saw, large table saw, and drill press is very helpful. Sometimes two or more wooden boat owners or woodworkers can get together to share the cost of purchasing of tools, or the maintenance or rental of a well-equipped wood shop.

Wet-and-dry shop vacuum

Clamp lights

Extension cords

Portable-radio

Portable electric fan

Multi-tool - (electric chisel, sander)

Don't try to fit all into one toolbox. Plastic five-gallon buckets are excellent for carrying tools and are easy to pull up on deck with a rope handle and a rope when the boat is hauled out.

If you've decided to do your own work, then you might as well start collecting these tools with the money you'll save by doing the work yourself. Chances are that if you enjoy this kind of work, you may, I hope, use these tools over and over again to fix other wood boats. There are a lot of them and they all need work. Even if you never work on another boat besides your own, with these tools you will be able to repair and maintain your own boat anytime, anywhere.

THE USE OF WOOD PRESERVATIVE

A short note about the use of fungicidal bedding compounds and poisonous wood preservatives such as pentachlorophenol (penta or PCP) and cuprinol:

I am opposed to these dangerous chemicals being used anywhere in the interior or living spaces aboard a boat. A much better and longer lasting method of preventing fungal growth and deterioration of wood can be achieved by painting and bedding all bare wood, *especially seal all end-grain,* that is used in con-

31

struction or reconstruction and by good boat-keeping practices, such as providing proper ventilation below and by not allowing any fresh water leaks to enter the hull from the deck, cabin, or leaky plumbing. Wood boats rot from the deck down.

If you still feel compelled to use additional wood preservatives in the interior of the boat, an excellent long-lasting alternative can be made by using a mixture of beeswax and corn oil, heated up to a paste wax in a tin can. The proportions are about ⅓, beeswax, ⅔ corn oil, or adjust to desired thickness. Beeswax and corn oil are both fungicidal and will kill and prevent the growth of mold, bacteria and fungus, and waterproof wood—and, this mixture is safe for humans. This mixture is especially good for applying on wooden masts or any bare wood to prevent fresh water absorption. It can be applied to fuzzy wood that forms on unpainted wood in engine rooms or other areas of high humidity and poor ventilation.

Another good product that kills mold and prevents rot is cedar oil, available on the internet called "Cedarcide" in a bug sprayer will kill mold and chase away insects. Spraying the interior of your wood boat regularly with vinegar or one gallon of vinegar to one bottle of peroxide will kill mold and fungus that promotes rot. Always ventilate all parts of your wood boat.

Contrary to popular use, linseed oil should ***never*** be used on bare wood as it rapidly turns black and grows mold and fungus. On several large schooners today, Vaseline and linseed oil are applied to their masts. Petroleum products such as "Vaseline" should ***never*** be used on bare wood since petroleum dissolves the lignum, a natural wood glue that hold the wood fibers together. Fill all checks and cracks in solid masts with beeswax to prevent fresh water, termites and wood-borers from entering. Install cypress stop-waters sloping upwards on any mast checks right above the mast boot to prevent freshwater from following the check below deck.

TERMITES

Are a real danger to wood boats. Although some woods, teak, cypress are more resistant to termites. At the first sign of termite poop, wings or swarming on windless evenings steps must be taken to remove them. Subterranean termites leave a muddy trail and can do tremendous damage in a very short time. Tenting and fumigating your boat, although expensive is the only way to eradicate termites. And then repair the damage they create. Don't wait. Tent either in or out of the water as soon as you can. And tent again if termites return.

THE USE OF PLYWOOD

Although plywood seems to be initially ideal and quite strong for some repairs, it is short-lived and because of all the thirsty, kiln-dried end-grain exposed on all edges, it is prone to delamination and rot. If any of the conditions for rot are resent rot will occur.

If plywood must be used, especially for decking or bulk-heads, use a good grade of marine plywood, seal the end-grain and all surfaces well with epoxy and cover with a generous layer of epoxy and fiberglass mat, and non-skid paint on deck.

3

HAULING OUT

It is essential to haul a wood boat out once a year. Immediately prior to the haul, empty bilge water, especially if fouled with oil and fuel. The forces of water pressure are from the outside-in when the boat is in the water. If it is hauled with a lot of water in its bilge, the water pressure is opposite; the caulking is not designed to withstand this pressure. If any caulking is to be done, it will be more difficult to do a satisfactory job if the seams are wet or holding water or waste oil.

METHODS OF HAULING

There are two main methods of hauling out. One is in a cradle on a railway or elevator, the other is in a travel-lift. The rail or elevator is much gentler on the hull. Make certain that the lift operator is familiar with the vessel's underwater shape. Show him a photo or line drawing. It is also helpful to have some reference marks on the hull or to remember such things as where the forefoot turns into the keel, where the rudder begins, where the transducer or knot-log spinner is, where the bulkheads, struts and props are.

It is also very important that you are there while your boat is being hauled. The operator of the travel lift or winch is the captain of the situation and has had more experience at this than you (you hope) so be respectful. However, nobody cares for your boat as much as you do, so you are there to supervise the procedure and to protect your interest.

After you are sure that the belly straps of the travel-lift are in the correct position so as not to crush the transducer, knot log, prop, rudder or any other appendages, check to see that the operator ties the straps together so they don't slip up the forefoot with sufficient rope and a good holding knot. The straps should be placed near bulkheads or bridge-decks to resist the great compression loads. Make wooden wedges to fit under the rub rails to reduce compression.

High-pressure pressure washers used at a boatyard can damage wet wood, can remove wood plugs and can blow out caulking. Rent a low-pressure pressure washer and use it carefully or scrub and clean the bottom while the boat is still in the water.

If there is a lot of room in the yard, have the operator put your boat in the shade of a shed or tree or facing East and West so that the sun passes directly over the deck and does not shine on the sides of the hull. Check that there is a good, hard surface under the boat. It is easier to keep it clean. If it is asphalt, check the other boats to see if their screw jack supports are sinking into it from their own weight. If so, place plywood pads below the side supports before they are tightened, especially if the boat is very heavy. As the operator lowers the boat, his assistant will select the proper keel blocks to place under the keel.

Have them block the boat so that the waterline is level to the ground. This will help the deck to drain rainwater; otherwise, the water will all puddle up in the bow and not drain through the scuppers. Many a boat has been broken by badly placed keel blocks. Make sure that the keel goes down evenly on the keel blocks and that the one in the middle is not higher than the rest. This can result in broken floor timbers, broken keelsons, loose garboards, and can even hog a vessel or break its back. Then check to see if the boat is standing up straight and not leaning to one side. Almost all of the entire weight of the boat should be on the keel blocks, but if the boat is leaning, there may be too much force on the side supports. The screw jacks or side supports should be placed with angles square to the hull.

Keel blocks should not be in the way of the keelbolts, the wormshoe, or the rudder, if these need to be replaced. If keel blocks have to be in the way of an area where you need to work, place short keel blocks with wedges driven on top of them from each side to make up the height difference so the wedges can be removed one at a time and the keel blocks moved one at a time to work underneath. (Chapter 17, Figure 85)

The popular method of shoring at the yards is with four screw jacks. Ask the foreman or operator if you can have at least four jacks for each side; this will support the turn of the bilge more evenly, and help the boat retain her shape during the haul-out. This is especially important if replacing planks or framing, or replacing rubrails, caulking, or any other structural work. The screw jacks should be placed near the bulkheads, have large plywood pads, and not over-tightened, as this can distort the hull and may even break frames.

If the boat has an overhanging counter or bow, like Rhodes, Fife, Alden, or Herreshoff-designed sailboats, place additional supports under the forefoot and counter. These can be screw jacks or 4 x 4 shores with wooden wedges and pads. This should be done immediately after the boat is hauled to stop deformation or sagging of the ends. Wooden boats need to be hauled and blocked correctly.

SETTING UP A WORK SPACE

Having satisfactorily blocked the vessel, you can begin to make this area more comfortable for the work that needs to be done. Hose down the area so it is clean; you will clean up at the end of each haul-out day. This will help to keep a good working attitude, improve the quality of your work, and keep your tools clean and easy to find. Make it a rule never to put your tools on the ground and always to remove your shoes before going below. Tie the boarding ladder securely to a stanchion or chain plate. Make two tables out of wooden doors, plywood, or planks supported on steel drums or sawhorses: one for tools, one for a work table. The tools should be organized into painting-related tools, such as scrapers, brushes, sanders, and sandpaper (in plastic bags), carpentry hand tools, and power tools. Only the tools that will be needed that day should be out on the tool table. The work table should be kept clean and all tools returned to the tool table when not in use. On the work table, there should be a vise and a hand or electric bench grinder. Now the staging and scaffolding can be moved over to the boat. Rent scaffolding or build it yourself if the yard doesn't provide it or use 2 x 12s on 55-gallon drums or saw horses. Bring enough scaffolding to go all around the boat. Create a workspace that makes it easy to work as efficiently as possible. Any compromise that you make early in the game will stay with you for the entire haul-out.

COVERS AND SHEDS

Planking and caulking a wooden boat are best done during the rainy season when the moisture content in the wood is high. A simple cover over the booms, peaked by a topping lift or halyard so that it drains well, is adequate for short-term haul-outs. If a long-term reconstruction or restoration is planned, it will be necessary to provide more protection for yourself and the boat. Removing the masts may be necessary if the boat is to be placed in a covered shed. If there is no shed available, a simple frame and cover can be constructed. The frame can be made out of bamboo, bent steel, conduit steel, water pipe and pipe fittings, 2 x 2s or 2 x 4s, or PVC pipe. Canvas, plastic, plywood, corrugated steel or fiberglass panels can be used over the frame. If a canvas or plastic tarp is used as a cover over a frame, provision must be made for reinforcement at chafe and tie-down areas. Provide adequate ventilation and lighting.

AVOID USING FRESH WATER TO CLEAN DECKS

Whether your boat is in the water or hauled, continued use of fresh hose water to clean the deck will cause your wooden boat to rot. After rain, bucket salt water over the deck. It's best to use salt water and Joy (mixes well with salt water) to clean the deck. If you are concerned about your boat drying out while hauled, rig up a pump that pumps salt water to your deck. If your wooden boat is where there is no salt water, mix a mild solution of salt and water. If you notice deck or cabin leaks, sprinkle rock salt until you can fix them.

4

THE SURVEY

By the time the boat is blocked, the scaffolding set up, and the work and tool tables made, the day is pretty well over. Take some time to look over the hull so you can plan the work ahead. If you do not feel confident enough to do the survey, hire a professional surveyor who knows wooden boats. If you will survey your own boat, here are a few things to look for:

SURVEYING A WOOD BOAT

The first inspection is done by eye and nose. First walk all the way around the boat, looking for irregularities, wet seams, unfairness, cracks in the planks, hard spots, wet butt blocks, wetness between the ballast keel and hull. Mark wet spots with chalk or paint. To find unsound areas which appear to be in good condition, it is necessary to sound the boat gently with a hammer or mallet.

Unsound areas will make a dull or hollow sound when hit with a mallet. Watch for areas that are wet or bruised, where paint does not stick well or rust streaks coming from a plank seam, the keel joint or a butt block. Hold your other hand on the hull near where you are sounding to feel for loose planking or timbers.

When an unsound area is discovered, probe with an awl or ice pick very carefully. Do not make any unnecessary holes in the wood as they are possible places where marine borers can enter. Circle with chalk or crayon any holes you make with a probe so they can be filled with epoxy putty or bottom paint thickened with cement if the areas probed are not otherwise replaced or repaired.

• *Bondo or other polyester putties should never be used on a wooden boat.*

Use your nose in the interior of the boat to smell for mold or rot. Wood rot deterioration will be found at areas of poor drainage on deck, poorly ventilated areas, especially at the stem or stern, behind butt blocks, between sawn frames, behind stringers, between bulkheads and frames at floor timbers, near iceboxes under sinks, under cockpits, under ceilings, at the tops of frames, at cabin corner posts, under and around sliding hatches, between deck and cabin, under chain plates, around scuppers, water tanks, where electrical wires enter deck, around showers and anywhere under where there are cabin top or deck leaks.

• *Wood boats rot from the deck down.*

Look at the bow or anywhere for short planks. If there are

many of these, it may indicate that the stem was replaced, or improper repairs were made. *There is no acceptable reason for having short planks at the bow or anywhere else on the boat.* They weaken the entire structure. Even if these appear to be in good shape, you should plan to gradually replace them with longer planks.

Sometimes boats are designed to suit a specific condition for the area where they are used. For example, boats built on the East Coast have steeper or higher bows and have more sheer than those built on the West Coast of the United States. This is because the nature of the seas of the Atlantic, Caribbean, and the Gulf of Mexico are short and choppy, so additional sheer and high bows allow for more buoyancy and drier decks.

Some of the fishing boats built for use in the Pacific Northwest have opening doors and ports only on the starboard side. This is because the prevailing weather comes from the nor'west and you wouldn't want a door or window opening to a breaking sea. These boats are designed for beating to weather up the coast. Some commercial fishing boats, Montereys especially, may even have an extra plank on the port side or higher bulwarks to port, for the same reason.

Before making any major changes in a boat that is new to you, consider the reasons for the original design. There is more evolution and design consideration in the traditional wooden boat than we may ever be aware of, so before you make any changes in a boat, test it and live with it the way it is. You may change it and later discover that it was better off the way it was before the change.

Initial Dry-out

As soon as the boat is out of the water, it will begin to dry out. Look for places that remain wet: along seams, at butt blocks, or around fasteners. Take a piece of chalk, paint or crayon and circle these areas so you can find them after they dry out. Check wet seams and especially all butt blocks for cotton with a pocket knife. Lot of times the caulker took off for lunch or the weekend and came back without marking where he left off. It is customary to find seams totally without cotton caulking in an otherwise cotton-caulked hull.

Worms

Worms can enter a boat through the seams, at places where the bottom paint has been chipped off, around through-hull fittings, under rudders, at rudderposts, behind the ballast keel, and in the deadwood. Any hole or wet spot on the planking should be inspected and circled with chalk. Worm damage that goes less than ½-way through the plank can be burned out with a hand-held torch and filled with cement or epoxy. Where worm damage is extensive, the plank should be replaced. Cypress is very worm resistant. Worms just love fir, and especially oak. I've seen worms in teak planking and worms eat through fiberglass to get at plywood core of rudders. Renew antifouling paint every year.

Corrosion

Prop, shaft, rudder hardware, and keel coolers should be examined for pitting or discoloration; worn out zincs should be renewed. Do not over-zinc your boat as this may cause more, rather than less corrosive action to occur and damage adjacent wood. If the prop, strut, underwater fitting, or through-hull is red, pink or pitted, strike it with a hammer. It should ring, not thud dully, or crumble.

Fairness and Hard Spots

Look carefully at the shape of the hull and feel with your hand for hard spots or any places that do not form a fair curve. Mark these areas with chalk. These hard spots may indicate several cracked or broken frames in a row. An angular area at plank edges is called chining and indicates broken frames in a row especially below chain plates at the turn of the bilge. They are also indicative of loose butt blocks, over-caulked seams, or deteriorated fasteners. Look particularly for unfairness at the turn of the bilge where the frames must make the tightest bends and are most likely to be broken. Check these places inside the hull by removing interior cabinets, etc., which can be easily removed and look to see if the planks are touching the frames.

Turn the hammer around and press the handle with your shoulder against any area that is not fair and at the butt blocks. Watch for movement and water coming from the plank seams when you put pressure on the hammer. This will indicate deteriorated fasteners or broken or rotted frames.

Do not gut the boat if broken or rotten frames are discovered without. considering the alternative methods for replacing them. If you decide to remove part of the interior to gain access to these areas, be delicate: remove wood plugs and back out screws carefully. The most expensive, time consuming and skilled part is the reconstruction of interior cabinetwork and joinery, so take your time, number each part and draw diagrams to help reassemble it when the structural work is completed. Take photos with your cellphone if you have to. If the frames are broken but not rotten, sister frames may be added near the old ones. Sometimes this can be done from the deck by removing the covering board. With the covering board removed, steam bent frames may be driven down into place without disturbing the interior. Sometimes, several planks can be removed to allow sister frames to be inserted from the outside and to enable clamps to be used through these spaces to hold the frames together and in place while they are being fastened. This method is used where ceilings are in the way or if access is being blocked by permanently installed tanks or machinery.

Examine the planks by running your hand over them as you did when checking for hard spots; this time check for outward cupping at the edges of the planks. This is a sure sign that refastening is needed. Wet seams can also indicate this condition, it will do no good to caulk an area where the fasteners are deteriorated and no longer holding. Addition of more caulking in these unsound areas will just drive the planks further apart and cause more leaking when the boat is back in the water.

Wet or leaky garboards will not be cured by over-caulking. If they are leaking at the lower edge, suspect keel bolt deterioration. To remove excess cotton in the seams, raise the hull to take the compression load on the garboard seams and pull out the caulking, try lifting the boat up under the turn of the bilge.

A long 2 x 8 plank on top of three or four screw jacks placed under the turn of the bilge can gently raise the boat to take the pressure off the garboard seams. Reef out all the cotton and seam compound. Then ease the boat down on its keel blocks. Add additional, or if soft, replace the floor timbers, with wings rising up the floor timbers close to the turn of the bilge. Additional keelbolts through the new beefy floor timbers may also help. Refasten or replace the garboards, fasten them to the new floor timbers and caulk them properly.

Using a plastic mallet or hammer with masking tape over the head to avoid denting or cracking the paint above the waterline, tap the planking gently especially at the butts, where the planks meet the transom, and at the stem. Any suspected loose planks, press the plank with the back of the hammer handle, with your other hand feel if the plank being pressed is moving because it is loose, look for water squeezing out when pressed.

Fasteners

Pull some fasteners each side in different locations to determine their condition. Iron nails and ring-shank nail heads need to be exposed with a chisel so you can remove them with a cat's paw or vise grip and pry bar. Be careful not to damage or crush the surrounding area too much: use wooden pads under hammers and pry bars when prying against the hull. Sometimes it is necessary to drive nail fasteners in a little bit farther to break their hold before attempting to remove them. Inspect the bolts at the butt blocks and replace these where needed. If removing an iron nail fastened plank and replacing it, you can do more damage to the frames by prying out the nail. Remove the caulking, use a hole saw around the nail, remove the plank and hacksaw or angle grinder or Sawzall off the nail flush with the frame and fasten the new plank to avoid the sawed-off nail.

Remove copper rivets from the inboard side. Remove the washer inboard. Remove the wood plug outboard and hammer the rivet through to the outside with a punch. Examine the rivet for pink metal indicating electrolysis. Put one end of the rivet in a vise or vise-grip, and with another vise-grip, try to bend the rivet stem. It should bend without breaking or turning into powder. If it is brittle, breaks, or powders, the rivets will need replacing. Iron keel bolts are always suspect and never last very long.

Remove bronze screws for inspection. If they shear off or crumble, replace them. If the boat is fastened with brass screws, replace them with silicon bronze screws. If a bronze or brass screw shears off while being removed, drill it out. Use an easy-out and vise grip to remove broken screws, or drill another hole beside it. Bronze screws last about 30 years in saltwater. The best material for planking fasteners is Monel. Or use wood "trunnels" to avoid metal corrosion.

STEMS, STEM FITTINGS, BOBSTAYS

Inspect the stem and around the bobstay fitting to make sure that there isn't rot or soft wood here due to metal corrosion or crushed wood fibers from collision with objects such as logs or docks. Deteriorated soft wood will appear either as cracks, rust marks, or flaky paint on the side of the stem near the waterline. These should be examined, carefully probe with an awl and inspect the fittings themselves for hairline cracks which indicate stress corrosion and impending failure. If the bobstay is at or near the waterline, it is in an area of accelerated electrolytic and galvanic action. If there is any question as to the condition of these fasteners or fittings at the bobstay, they should be removed, inspected and, if necessary, replaced. The bobstay fasteners should be of the same type of metal as the bobstay itself.

Another type of corrosion occurs where stainless steel touches stainless steel. This is called "galling." It may appear as rust or tiny rusty surface cracks and can be eliminated by isolating or insulating two stainless steel fittings by using sturdy non-metallic bushings or washers between them. Bronze can be used for fittings if no other iron or steel is in the immediate vicinity.

A type of corrosion exists whereby dissimilar metals corrode when in the presence of fast-moving salt water. This type of corrosion is also very often found at bobstay or other waterline fittings. Corrosion of the metals causes chemical reactions which can deteriorate the surrounding wood, leaving the metals apparently unaffected.

Where bobstay fittings are through-bolted to the inside of the stem, a large hardwood back-up plate or *apron* should be installed and large fender washers of the same metal be placed under the nuts. Never just bolt through a one-piece stem, without using a large, well-bedded back-up pad with well-sealed end grain.

Use bedding compound between the fitting and the wood of the stem, and a gasket made of painted canvas or tar paper bedded on both sides to insulate the wood from deteriorating under the fitting.

Eyebolts or lag eyes should never be used as bobstay fittings. They are not sufficient for sustaining the tremendous rigging loads or impact loads from collision with waterline objects. Eyebolts weaken the stem by point loading and may cause the wood through which they are fastened to split or crack. The bobstay fitting should have a large enough base to distribute the load and to contain strong through-bolts or stout hanger bolts.

If a shackle is used to attach the bobstay to the bobstay fitting, this shackle bolt or pin should be seized with wire. Galvanized steel shackles last longer than stainless steel ones. Coat the threads of the shackle bolt with good waterproof grease (without graphite). Avoid using the type of shackle that has a cotter pin securing the bolt; especially avoid cotter pin shackles for rigging anchor gear as the tiny cotter pin is often the weakest point. *Don't use cheap stainless steel chain made in China for bobstays or Chinese stainless steel anchor chain.* Use American-made high-tensile galvanized chain and galvanized shackles, replace it when it rusts. Put the turnbuckle under the bowsprit, not at the waterline.

BOWSPRITS

Raise inboard section of bowsprits above deck to ventilate underside and prevent rot. Never mount a bowsprit directly on deck. Installing a bow roller anywhere except close to bow may break bowsprit or transmit anchor loads to rig or may break bobstay fittings if electric anchor winch pulls too tight after anchor is raised. Seal underside of bowsprit and all end-grain.

RUDDERS

Check the bottom of the rudder for worm damage. Next check the forward edge of the rudderpost and aft edge of deadwood or sternpost for worm damage and where the rudder goes through the deadwood. Inspect the rudder bearings for excessive wear; push on the side of the rudder to determine if there is lateral movement. If they are very sloppy, the gudgeons, pintles, and bottom bearing may need to be taken to a machine shop to be filled and re-drilled. Sometimes if the fittings cannot be removed, a block of Teflon can be sculpted to fit into a gudgeon that is elongated due to excessive wear. It can then be re-drilled for the pintle. PVC pipe can be used if necessary. The rudder should not flex if you push on it. If there are gaps between the boards of the rudder or if it is not very strong, the through-bolts must be exposed and examined for deterioration. *Brass should never be used underwater* since it is made of copper and zinc, and the zinc corrodes very quickly leaving voids and weakening the metal severely. This type of corrosion is called dezincification. Use silicon bronze, Monel, Aquamet shafting, or #316 grade stainless steel, for underwater fittings.

Iron drifts, which are often used to assemble rudders, should be examined. If they are badly rusted, making a new rudder is usually the best repair.

KEELBOLTS

Keelbolts are probably the highest-stressed, most critical fasteners in a ballast keel sailboat. These should be inspected every haul-out for looseness and signs of deterioration. The best time to inspect the keelbolts is when the boat is out of the water and the entire weight of the vessel is on the keel. Sometimes the keelbolts just need to be re-tightened, especially if they were recently installed or never re- tightened. Use a hammer and cold chisel or large screwdriver to try to spin the washer under the nut to determine if the washer is loose. If the washer will spin or turn, the keelbolt needs to be retightened, is broken, has corroded through or stretched. Usually the nut is corroded onto the threads of the bolt and will need some lubrication or heat to free it. Use a deep socket of the correct size and a breaker bar or large ratchet with a cheater-pipe fitted over the handle for more leverage to tighten the nut. If the iron keelbolt nuts are too misshapen or corroded to use a socket wrench on them, they will need to be cold-chiseled, sawzalled, or cut-torched off and the keelbolt replaced.

Usually the condition of the nut will give a pretty fair indication of the condition of the rest of the keelbolt. Keeping the bilge dry will prolong the life of the keelbolts. If there are fresh water deck leaks, find out where they are and eliminate them. The addition of rock salt to the bilge water will also rapidly corrode the keelbolts. If the bolt turns with the nut or if the bolt unthreads from its hole in the floor timber, keel, or keelson, then the keelbolt is corroded through, or the nut may be completely deteriorated or missing from the bottom end of the keelbolt.

Keelbolt Survey

Keelbolts are usually good for about 20-30 years in salt water, sometimes more. Wet seams or rust streaks between the timbers of the deadwood in the area of a keelbolt indicate a deteriorated or loose keelbolt. If any of the keelbolts are bad, it will be the first or forward-most one. Tapping on the keelbolt with a hammer tells little about its condition. A much more positive method of surveying keelbolts is to have them X-rayed by a mobile X-ray unit. This is quite expensive but will give an accurate picture of their condition. Usually it will suffice to X-ray only one or two to get an idea of the condition of the others. It is a good idea to X-ray the keelbolt that is under the engine if there is one there. Even if the keelbolts were replaced, there is a chance that this one was overlooked or left for when the engine needed to be pulled out for rebuilding and may never have been replaced.

The very best way to determine their condition is to pull one you suspect may be deteriorated. If the keelbolts need replacing, you may decide to replace the worst ones this haul-out, the ones that are leaking, or every other one now, and do the remaining ones next haul-out. That way you have a whole year to get it together, collect the right materials and by replacing every other one this time, you won't have to worry about the keel falling off right away.

HOGGING

Keel Hog

Hogging is a condition where the ends of the boat sag or the shear humps up by way of the chainplates on a sailboat or midship on a powerboat. On traditional cargo boats, that have no ballast keel, the cargo hold must be kept in ballast when the cargo is off-loaded. The internal ballast must replicate the weight of the cargo to prevent the hull from distortion. Before any re-planking is done, the hog should be removed by replicating the weight of the cargo in the cargo hold and if necessary installing a ballast shoe or metal fabricated channel bolted to the bottom of the keel to straighten or reverse the hog.

Sheer Hog

Where sheer hog is observed on a wood sailboat with turnbuckles, the first step is to remove the turnbuckles and install deadeyes and lanyards to isolate the rig loads from the hull. Look for broken frames along the lower end of the chainplates. This usually accompanies sheer hog in a sailboat. The cure will be replacing the broken frames or sister framing, re-planking the topsides and removal and replacement of the sheer clamp or shelf if distorted. Install deadeyes and lanyards to act as shock absorbers to prevent future sheer hog. In the old days, nobody would think of using turnbuckles on a wood sailboat shrouds unless it was a racing boat never expected to last more than a few seasons. Turnbuckles were only used on steel-hulled sailing boats or aluminum or fiberglass.

ORGANIZING A PLAN OF ATTACK

First consider the list that you made from the survey. Decide which of these items needs to be done first. Rewrite the list in the numerical order of their priority. Then decide which of these things on the list you can realistically take care of at this time. What needs to be done immediately? What can wait until the next haul-out? How much will this cost? How much money have you got for the haul-out? How much time can you spare?

This part of the haul-out is most important. From it will emerge *organization.* It will ensure that you do not bite off more than you can chew. It is easier to tear your boat apart than it is to put it back together. This will take skill, time, money, and the right materials. Work on one project at a time and don't go on to another until the first one is completed. It is perfectly all right to replace the bad planks on one side of the boat now or the worst ones now and do the rest next year or reframe only one side at a time. It's okay to replace the first three keelbolts or every other one this time. Be realistic and organize the work starting with the ones that have the most priority. Many a boat has had to be abandoned and died at a boatyard because the owner tried to do too much all at one time. Revise your list and be clear about what you will be able to take care of this time.

Removal of Bottom Paint

If there is a heavy build-up of paint on the bottom, or the paint is cracked or peeling off in chunks it is probably time to grind the bottom down to bare wood and start adding bottom paint all over again. If soft antifouling paint has been used, and you are not happy with the way it rubs off when you scrub it underwater or if it goes away too quickly at the waterline, you may decide to use hard or vinyl bottom paint this time. If the boat is iron fastened, it is a good idea to use a barrier coat between the bare wood and the copper paint. You can use red lead, zinc chromate, or coal tar epoxy as a barrier coat. If you use coal tar epoxy, glue the first coat of bottom paint to the epoxy catalyzed tar while the last coat of coal tar is still sticky. If you will use a hard vinyl bottom paint you will not be able to use oil-based barrier coats since the vinyl thinners will dissolve the oil-based undercoats. In this case, you'll have to use an epoxy or vinyl red lead and/or a coal tar epoxy such as Tarset or Intergard Blackmastic. This will insulate the iron fasteners and iron keel from electrolysis with the copper in the paint.

Apply the first coat of any paint onto bare wood thinly so it absorbs into the wood, always read and follow the instructions on the can.

Use a soft-pad disc grinding with 24 or 36 grit resin-coated masonry sanding discs. Always hold the grinding disc flat to the surface. Using the edge will dent the wood.

If all the paint does not need to be removed, but only well

sanded for new paint, the loose paint should be scraped with a putty knife, wood scraper, or wire brush. Then the surface can be sanded with a soft pad grinder, or the old paint wet-sanded by hand with coarse, wet-and-dry sanding paper and water. This will make less paint dust.

You cannot paint hard bottom paint directly over soft or sloughing antifouling bottom paint. The solvents in the vinyl paint will dissolve the soft paint below it. Always make a test patch for adhesion and compatibility when switching to a different type of bottom paint. A simple test to determine if soft or hard antifouling paint was used is made by rubbing the paint with a rag soaked in mineral spirits. If soft oil-base paint was used, it will rub off on the rag. If vinyl or hard paint was used, it will not rub off on the rag.

If the bottom paint is good and not flakey or cracked, rub with a 3M abrasive pad and water to prepare it for repainting. Don't paint over flakey or cracked paint. It must be scraped off and feathered, or faired smooth, with soft pad and grinder and filled before repainting.

If no work needs to be done to the bottom besides painting, it is always a good idea to wash the surface with fresh water and an abrasive pad, then get the new paint on the bottom as soon as possible, before the old paint cracks and flakes off.

In these methods of bottom paint removal, extra care should be taken to protect yourself against chemical odors, smoke, and dust—all of which are very toxic. Wear protective clothing, gloves, goggles, and suitable respirator devices to protect yourself from the dangerous toxic and cumulative poisons in the antifouling paint.

5

REPLACING KEELBOLTS

PREPARATION FOR REMOVAL OF KEELBOLTS

In preparation for replacing the keelbolts, it is a good idea to secure a large enough section of pipe or PVC over the nut and upper end of the keelbolt. Place a bead of bedding compound around the outside bottom edge of the pipe and fill the cylinder up with penetrating oil. Automatic transmission fluid mixed with diesel, kerosene or paint thinner makes the best penetrating and lubricating oil. With these pipes fitted and sealed over the top of each keelbolt and filled with penetrating oil, hopefully some of it will find its way down along the bolt and free the corrosive bond long before you attempt to break the bolt free from its hold on the keel. This can even be done while the boat is still in the water as long as the keelbolts are not leaking. In that case, it should be done immediately after haul-out. Check the level of the penetrating oil occasionally and refill the cylinder if necessary.

Types of Keels

Ballast keels can be lead, iron, and sometimes cement—with or without chunks of iron or steel imbedded in it. (This can be anything from old boiler punchings to window or elevator weights, chunks of lead, tire weights or railroad track).

Lead keels—Keelbolts for a lead keel should be silicon bronze, never brass or naval bronze. Stainless steel (316-grade) and good Aquamet stainless steel propeller shafting can also be threaded up for keelbolts. Bronze keelbolts can be freed up, tightened, and occasionally easily removed. Avoid hammering directly on the end of the keelbolt; this will increase the diameter of the end of the bolt and make it nearly impossible to drive it down, or up through the keel. The hole in the bottom of the keel must be located and the wooden plug or compound removed. Sometimes there are inspection plugs on the side of the keel over the lower end of the keelbolt and nut. (This is especially the case in iron keels where a shorter bolt means less surface to corrode to the keel and tends to make extraction a little easier.) Keelbolts with side holes in the keel will need to be removed and installed from the inside of the boat. Use a hydraulic jack to remove the bolts, jack them preferably from the bottom-up, or if necessary from the top-up.

Sometimes keelbolts are threaded directly into the top of the lead keel. Hole are drilled and threaded, extending six to eight times the diameter of the bolt into the top of the keel. If this is done, antimony is added to the top of the lead keel when it is formed to harden the lead so it can be drilled and tapped to hold the bolt.

Keelbolts are sometimes cast directly into the lead keel. If this has been done, and the original keelbolts have deteriorated, it will be necessary to drop the keel a bit or to cut the bolts off between the deadwood and the keel with a sawzall and metal cutting blade if they can't be removed, leaving enough to jack or twist out.

The upper part of the keelbolt that was cut off at the top of the ballast keel can then be removed by prying it up through its hole or left. A new hole can be drilled through the new floor timbers if they need to be removed or are deteriorated. New bolt holes will be added for the new keelbolts. When drilling through lead, kerosene can be used to help lubricate the drill bit. Floor timbers should be at least as thick as three times the diameter of the keelbolt. So if increasing the diameter of the keelbolt, it may also be necessary to increase the thickness of the floor timber.

Concrete keels—Concrete keels with cast-in-place bolts are a major problem, especially if there are pieces of steel cast in with the cement which is usually the case. Drilling through the cement will be hard enough with a masonry bit however, the cutter at the end of the bit will break off when it hits the steel imbedded in the cement and a high-speed metal bit must replace the masonry bit until the steel is drilled through, then back to the new masonry bit. Never set the automatic drill button when drilling through a cement keel, because when the drill bit hits a piece of steel, the drill will stop turning the drill bit and start turning the driller. It may be necessary to scrap the original concrete keel and cast up another concrete keel with through holes for replaceable keelbolts.

Iron keels—When removing keelbolts in iron keels that go through the keel to the bottom or to inspection holes in the side of the keel, it will be necessary to soak the top of the bolts in penetrating oil prior to their attempted removal. Wear leather gloves whenever you are removing iron or steel keelbolts from an iron keel. Remove the plug from the lower end to expose the nut.

Use a hydraulic jack from below to break loose the friction hold of the keelbolt on the iron keel. Remove the nut and position the hydraulic jack with a smaller nut or section of rod slightly smaller than the diameter of the keelbolt on top of the jack squarely under the bottom end of the keelbolt. Raise the jack until it takes the load. Then keep jacking and swapping the sections of rod. When using the jack under the keelbolt it may be necessary to check or tighten the wedges under the side supports so that the boat is not knocked over. Don't forget to loosen the wedges before you take pressure off the jack. Generally, the more deteriorated the iron or steel keelbolt, the easier it will be to remove it. Pry the top part out first if it is completely corroded, then jack the lower half up from the bottom.

If the floor timber through which the keelbolt passes is also deteriorated, split it out, replace the washer and nut on the top of the bolt and use a pipe wrench or vise grip placed below the washer. Then a hydraulic jack may be used under the vise grip or pipe wrench to raise the keelbolt up through its hole. If the top of the bolt is too deformed to replace the nut, weld a steel bar onto the top of the keelbolt so that it extends in front of and behind the keelbolt. Then use two hydraulic jacks simultaneously under the steel bar to jack the keelbolt straight up through its hole without bending it. As soon as pressure is taken up on the jacks, hammer the top of the keelbolt and place a jack on the bottom of the keelbolt at the same time. (Figure 5)

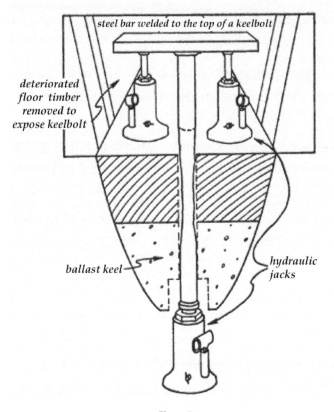

Figure 5
Removing a keelbolt with hydraulic jacks

Try everything, more pressure on the hydraulic jack, apply more penetrating oil, switch brands, try turning the keelbolt while jacking on it, take a break, try the next one, leave the jacks under it all night, and soak around the keelbolt with penetrating oil. It is always better to jack the bolt up and into the boat than to beat down on it with a sledge hammer from above and mushroom out the top of the bolt so it won't fit through the hole.

After all that trouble, you may decide to use Monel for keelbolts so that this same situation will not occur again in your lifetime. Check at the boatyards, prop shops, and scrap metal yards for Monel shaft. A propeller shop will be best equipped to thread up the ends for nuts. Special order the nuts or machine them out of square Monel stock. Make washers by drilling a hole through a quarter, fifty cent piece, or a silver dollar depending on the size of the bolt that is used. These coins are made out of the same metals as Monel: nickel and copper. The threads of the keelbolts should extend past where the nuts will tighten on them so that the nuts can be retightened later when everything compresses, or after the keelbolts stretch a little. Although common 304 stainless steel should not be used for keelbolts, propeller shafting stainless steel or #316 grade stainless can be used with good results.

Paint a canvas or caulking cotton washer with red or white lead or other bedding compound and place under the flat washer at the bottom end of the keelbolt. Place bedding compound, roofing tar, Irish felt or red or white lead and a canvas gasket under the new floor timber to prevent bolt leaks. Don't use all-thread or threaded rod as the threads are a path for water to leak along the bolt and a threaded rod is weaker, and corrodes faster, than a solid rod with threaded ends. Steel should not be used for keelbolts as they will deteriorate quickly.

Coat keelbolts with waterproof grease (non-graphite), roofing tar, polysulfide, or polyurethane caulking or bedding compound before installing. Lubricate the nuts with a good thread compound, white lead, tar, or waterproof grease. *Don't use any grease or Never Seize that contains graphite under salt water. Graphite is one of the most noble of all metals and will under salt water accelerate corrosion of metal on which it is applied.*

There should be at least five keelbolts of adequate size to hold the keel. Tighten them as tight as you can with the aid of a breaker bar, socket and cheater pipe. Tighten them again after everything has settled and re-tighten them again after the first hard sail. They should be re-tightened and the nuts checked for corrosion yearly.

Usually they are installed slightly off-set to minimize the possibility of splitting the wood through which they are fastened. Sometimes the considerate builder will insert wooden plugs in the side of the wooden keel to mark where the keelbolts are located. The holes in the bottom or side of the keel should be covered with wooden plugs or epoxy putty. Enter in the ship's log the date of any keelbolt replacement as well as the type, location, and material used.

Sandblasted or grind down to remove flakey paint. Paint immediately with red lead or epoxy paint or use coal tar epoxy. It is important to use a barrier coat between the iron of the keel and the copper in the bottom paint. The barrier coating must be applied immediately after sandblasting, a freshly sandblasted keel will begin to rust overnight.

6

FRAMING

If re-planking or refastening, first you must determine the condition of the frames. The frames are the main structure of the hull and they must be in good condition to hold the new and old fasteners securely. There are three types of frames: sawn, steam bent and laminated.

SURVEYING FRAMES

Sawn Frames

In order to replace sawn frames, first mark the shape of the curve of the inside of the hull on a wide board of the required thickness and suitable grain. Then cut out the curve with a circular saw or band saw to the greatest bevel and the bevels adjusted to fit the curve of the hull. Fit the outboard side of the frame to the hull by duplicating the correct bevels or angles so that the frame will fit tightly against the planking.

If you live near a beach or forest, see if you can find a crook or naturally curved piece of hardwood that corresponds to your template. Check for worm holes indicating borer infestation and remove bark and sapwood before shaping this grown crook to fit.

It is usually impossible to cut the entire frame out of one board—especially the ones in the middle of the vessel. So the frames are made of two or more sections of frame that overlap each other and are then joined together by several through-bolts. This framing method is usually found in larger boats where their scantlings prohibit the use of steam bent frames which are usually two inches by two inches or smaller. (Figure 6)

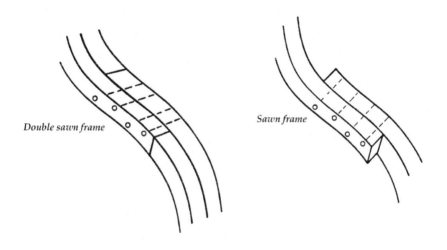

Figure 6

If this method is to be used, it is important that the overlapping areas or joints do not occur in the same place in adjacent frames. (Figure 7, 8 and 9)

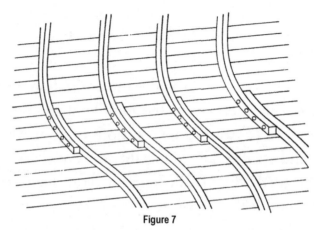

Figure 7
Joints of adjacent sawn frames should never fall on the same planks, as they do here.

This may cause the frames to 'work' or flex. Eventually, as the through-bolts corrode, the adjacent planks will be forced away from the frames. This usually occurs at the turn of the bilge, and no amount of caulking will stop the leaking as the boat sails, works in a seaway, or compresses when going aground, or sits on its keel at a boatyard.

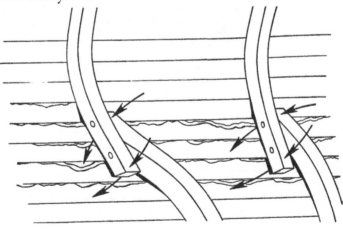

Figure 8
Here, planks are being forced away from the frames as the boat works and the frames flex.

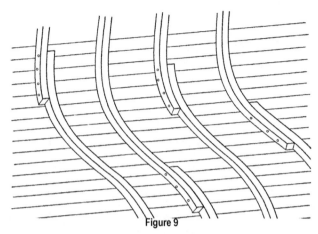

Figure 9

The right way. Stagger the joints in adjacent sawn frames. Afford a generous overlap (at least three planks) for each joint, and stagger the bolts so they are not all in the same line of grain.

If the wood is found to be good in the sawn frames, the bolts should be inspected for corrosion. These are usually steel, and if rusty, they should be replaced with silicone bronze or #316 grade stainless steel. If the rusty bolts have also deteriorated the surrounding wood, this wood will need to be replaced too. If the sawn frames are all joined along the same line, it may be necessary to install some full-length steam bent or laminated frames between them. This will restore continuity and stop the sawn frames from flexing and forcing the adjacent planks away from the frames. Check also for spaces between the frames and the planks. This will indicate that the frames are soft, are flexing or that the planking fasteners are no longer holding securely.

If the fasteners are deteriorated and the planks and frames are good, remove the fasteners, also remove the caulking in that area and wedge the planks back tightly against the frames before refastening. Clean out any wood shavings or debris between the frames and planks before re-fastening. Check for rot or soft wood near the through-bolts at the joints of double sawn frames, behind and along the sides of the frames, and behind stringers.

Steam bent Frames

These are usually found on boats smaller than 50 feet where a sawn frame of the same dimension would be too weak to use, and a sawn frame of adequate dimension would take up too much room inside the boat. Steam bent frames have less exposed end grain and for this reason, they are more resistant to rot than are sawn frames. They have a certain amount of locked-in pre-tensioning because they were steam bent and, because their grain follows their bend or is parallel to the bend, they are less easily broken than are sawn frames of the same dimension. When the boat is working or in compression, steam bent frames allow the hull to be more flexible.

Steam bent frames are generally made of white oak, due to oak's great ability to hold fasteners securely. Red oak is also widely used; however, red oak is much more susceptible to rot as its cellular open grain is tube-like and will absorb fresh water readily through its end-grain. White oak has closed cell grain like bamboo. Apitong and Ipe, locust and purple heart can be steam bent as can teak.

• *Seal the end-grain of any wood you put on your boat with paint or glue.*

It is better to use air-dried or green wood for steaming as it will bend more easily and is less brittle than kiln-dried wood.

But they will both work.

Check all the steam bent frames where they make radical curves for breaks which may occur on their outboard sides, between the frames and the planks. These cracks sometimes happen when the frame is originally being bent or while it is being fastened.

A cracked frame does not need to be removed, unless it is rotten or must be removed or partially removed to allow sprung planking to be wedged back into shape. It will usually suffice to install a full-length sister frame beside a cracked frame to regain the continuity lost by the cracked frame.

Check the fasteners at the floor timbers, as these are usually steel and can deteriorate the frame through which they are bolted. Check for rot or split frames near the deck or where they are bolted through a deck beam. Check also the sides of the frames and behind stringers for soft or mushy wood. Replace any deteriorated part of the frame with new wood, and fasten a sister frame nearby, or replace the entire frame. More about this later.

Alternate Steam bent and Sawn Frames

On some hulls there are sawn frames with alternate steam bent frames. This is typical of North Sea and Scandinavian built boats. The sawn frames are iron or copper nailed or bronze screwed, the steam bent frames are copper or iron riveted or clench nailed. Here, the sawn frames are for strength, and the much smaller steam- bent frames add continuity and allow the hull to be more flexible. Because of the rigidity of the sawn frame and the fact that the wood grain does not follow the direction of the curvature of the frame, sawn frames may break or their joints may work when subjected to sudden impact or compression loads. By their addition, steam bent frames act as shock-absorbers to reduce the sudden impact of compression loads that might otherwise damage the sawn frames. Here, the steam bent frames by themselves would be too weak because of their size to withstand the severe local conditions for which these boats were designed. The sawn frames are too rigid by themselves and do not offer continuous support from deck to keel or flexibility. The strength and rigidity of the sawn frame is complemented by the flexibility and continuity of the steam bent frame and together, they make a boat that is a little better suited for the rough conditions where it will be used.

A boat cannot be built that is rigid enough to resist working or flexing at sea. A few years ago *marine surveyors were warned never to proclaim a boat to be "seaworthy" since history has proven that no manmade boat or ship is truly worthy of the sea.*

The stronger and more rigid its construction, the more vulnerable it is to sudden enormous dynamic loading. Like the oak and the willow, it is more important that a wooden boat be flexible than over-rigid. In this type of alternate construction, examine the steam bent frames carefully for breaks or cracks because, just like the shock absorbers in your car, they do a lot of flexing, absorbing the sudden jolts that might otherwise cause damage to more rigid parts. Check the frames especially at the turn of the bilge. Boats designed for the North Sea and Scandinavian countries usually have very radical double curves which weaken steam bent and sawn frames.

Laminated Frames

By this process, a whole frame is built up of several laminations, glued to each other, and then the planking is fastened to it as though it were a single frame. This is by far the strongest method of the three framing types. Take a piece of wood, rip it into a bunch of strips, glue it back together with good epoxy, and it is stronger than the original piece of wood. It is necessary to use good glue and clamps. Use epoxy thickened with colloidal silica. Use any brand of epoxy that you have tested thoroughly. The laminations must be forced tightly against each other and against the planking. This type of framing is not usually found on original construction as the process of laminating the frames takes much more time than the other two methods if done correctly. It is excellent for repair where strength is needed or if it is impossible to get a steam bent frame behind a stringer or under an engine bed. This type of frame, if done correctly, will be very resistant to rot breaking or cracking and will probably outlast the other methods. To do a proper job of laminating frames, it may be necessary to steam bend the laminations to the appropriate curve. This will be explained in detail. Sometimes, a frame that is steam- bent will be ripped into two laminations to allow it to bend around a tight curve such as at the counter. They can be sawn partially through on each side to facilitate easier bending. When this is done, glue is not necessarily used. Do not confuse this type of steam bent frame with a broken or cracked frame. When looking at the side of a good laminated frame, you should not be able to see any spaces between the laminations or between the frame itself and the planking. It should appear as a solid, single frame of consistent dimension.

• *Never use plywood for laminating frames*

FRAME ACCESS

Access is a very important prerequisite to frame repair. It is ideal if the way can be cleared from the inside. All cabinetwork must be surgically removed, diagrams drawn, and parts numbered for reassembly. Leave all stringers for they may be helpful to you when installing the new frames. After access has been gained, examine the questionable frame or frames to determine the extent, nature, and cause of their deterioration.

REMOVING A BAD FRAME

If the frame is rotten, infested by termites, carpenter ants or severely broken or cracked, it must be removed. Remove enough of the ceiling or inside planking to inspect the questionable frame. Use a hole saw around the ceiling fasteners if nailed to avoid damaging the frame. With a circular saw, set to the depth of the frame, make several cuts across it about every eight inches. Care should be taken that the depth of the blade is set correctly and does not move. A sawzall (reciprocal saw) or saber saw can also be used. Take a sharp chisel, ½ inch or ¾ inch, and drive it into the frame between the horizontal cuts made by the saw and split out the pieces of frame until it is completely removed.

A large screwdriver can be used as you are destined to hit some fasteners with your chisel. Do not pry on the pieces of the frame; it is better to split them out in smaller pieces. Be careful not to pry or move the fasteners. After the frame is completely removed, go outside and find the corresponding plugs. Remove the plugs very carefully with a small screwdriver hammered into their centers twist and dig them out exposing the fastener head and leaving a clean hole. Then back out the screw, or if iron nails, hammer them out from the inside, being careful not to split the wood on the outside of the plug hole. A hardwood block with a hole drilled in it held over the plug hole from the outside will prevent splitting the wood around the plug hole and allow the fastener to be hammered out from the inside. In some cases, the nail or spike can be flushed off the outside of the frame with an angle grinder and cut-off wheel to avoid mutilating the frame by pulling it out with a crow bar.

After the old frame is removed clean up the inside of the planking with a sharp chisel and scraper. Fair the inboard side of the planking so that the new frame will be able to seat flat against the planks. The inboard side of the planking should be a smooth curve, not angular. Clean out all the mushy wood and dust with a vacuum cleaner. It will be a mess if there is loose dirt or dust anywhere near the epoxy.

FRAMING CONSIDERATIONS

The old frame has been removed, the fasteners backed or flushed off with a cut-off wheel and the area cleaned. Now you must decide which method you will use: steam bent, sawn, or laminated frames.

If *natural grown crooks* are to be used, remember that it is essential to remove all bark and sapwood, there must be no insect holes in the crooks, and if green or uncured, they must be aged or cured for one year for every inch of thickness or steamed one hour per inch. Grown crooks may cure a little faster if buried in mud, soaked in saltwater, or immediately if steamed.

If it was decided to remove the entire frame, then the entire frame must be replaced.

First consider the original frame. Was it oak? Was it red oak? White oak? Why did it rot or crack? Frames usually rot from deck leaks, leaking plumbing in the galley, leaks under a water tank, under an icebox, shower, or sink, always from fresh water, and from electrolysis or iron sickness.

You must consider what caused the deterioration. If from bad plumbing or deck leaks, these must be corrected as part of the frame repair or you haven't completed the job. Never just fix something, try to understand what caused the problem. Something obviously was wrong. There is not an endless supply of wood out there. A tree had to die for that wood you are using. Besides you can't keep fixing the same frame over and over again. You got the boat to use, to take you places on the water, so repair it right and get on with the rest of your life!

7

REPLACING A SAWN FRAME

MAKING A ROUGH TEMPLATE

Here's a quick way to make a template of the shape of the curve of the frame you need to replace:

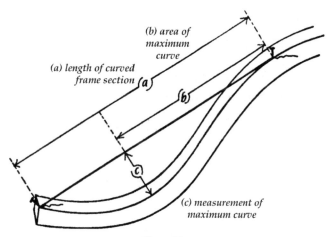

Figure 10

• Nail a length of string from the highest point of the frame, beside the one that needs replacing to the lowest point of that frame, so it is stretched tight.

77

• Measure the length of the string between the two nails and write down this measurement *(a)*.

• Measure from the top down to the part of the frame that is farthest away from the string line *(b)*. This is the point of maximum curve of the frame. Record this distance. (Figure 10)

• Now measure from here in to the frame *(c)*. This will tell you the maximum amount of curve there is in the frame. Record this measurement

• Find a piece of doorskin or ¼-inch plywood that is as long as the frame and is wider than the depth of the maximum curve plus the thickness of the frame.

• Draw on this piece the line that will represent the straight line of the string.

• Transfer the recorded measurements that describe the curve of the frame onto the plywood template.

• Use a flexible, wooden fairing batten to join the marks; now draw the curved line on the template.

• Cut the template out with a saber saw, circular saw or band saw.

MAKING THE FINISHED TEMPLATE

• Place this cut curved template against the planking on the hull where the new frame will go.

• Draw strike-up marks from the template onto the hull, holding the template to keep it from moving.

• Now examine the template to determine how far off it is from the curve of the hull. How far is it from fitting?

• There will be some "valleys" where there are spaces between the template and the hull. Measure the depth of the deepest valley and cut out a block of wood that is a little wider than that dimension and about 1½-inches long. The valley probably won't be wider than 1 inch.

• Holding the block of wood tightly against the hull, follow its curve, mark the template with a sharp pencil held close to where the block touches the template, thereby tracing the curve of the hull onto the template.

• Cut out the template with a saber saw or band saw close to the outside of the line, but *leave the line.* Sand or plane the template to the line.

• Place the template back up against the hull so that the strike-up marks line up. The template should now follow the curve of the hull. (Figure 11)

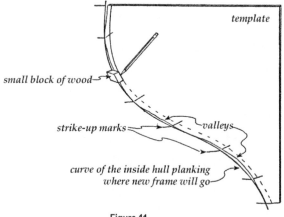

Figure 11

CHOOSING THE WOOD

If necessary, practice cutting this curved line on a scrap 2 x 6. Use a sharp blade. Since this curved template of the sawn frame really represents two pieces of frame joined together, mark on the template where you want to make the joint. Make sure it is not in the same place on the curve as the joint in the adjacent frames. Also allow for an overlap in the joint sufficient to fasten 3 or 4 good-sized through-bolts. The joint should span at least four planks. Measure the length of both parts of the frame and take the template to the lumberyard with you. Look through the wood till you find the right piece. Go to a boatyard or boatbuilder. Or the beach for driftwood. White oak, black locust, long-leaf yellow pine, whatever the boat was originally framed with. Lots of fishing boats and tugboats were originally framed with fir, or longleaf yellow pine, but the scantlings must be much greater when using fir or other pines because of the difference in strength between pine and white oak. Find a piece of wood whose grain follows the curve of the frame. This curved grain will strengthen the frame and also reduce the chances of the frame splitting especially when it is being fastened. It will also reduce the amount of exposed end-grain. Sometimes it is necessary to buy a large piece of wood and only use a small part of it. Make sure that there is no sapwood in the part of the board that is being used for the sawn frame. Sapwood is usually near the edge of the board and is usually a different and lighter color than the rest of the wood. Remember that the board must be at least as thick as the frame is wide. If you cannot find a board that is wide or thick enough, you may have to epoxy two or more boards together to make up one that will work.

After finding the right piece of wood, check the template once more. Reverse the template to the back side. Now nail it to the board. With a very sharp pencil held close to the edge of the template, mark it very carefully. If the board is too rough to mark on, plane or sand it smooth before fastening the template to it. After you mark the board, transfer the strike-up marks onto it from the template. Pull the nails and remove the template.

TAKING OFF THE BEVEL

Take the bevels. Place the template against the hull where the new frame will go. Mark one-foot intervals on the hull and on the template and mark the bevels between the template and the hull on the template at each station.

Compare and choose the greatest bevel from the bevels found and recorded at each station, select the most radical bevel (the angle with the greatest number of degrees over 90 degrees).

Set the saw blade to this bevel If the frame will be cut out on a band saw, saber saw, or circular saw, adjust the angle between the table and the blade of the saw to correspond with the greatest bevel. To do this be sure that the blade of the bevel gauge lays flat against the table of the saw and the saw blade is adjusted so that it is parallel to the handle of the bevel gauge.

Cut out the frame. The marks are transferred from the template or, if a form-fitting template was made, trace the outline of the template onto the board that will be the new frame. Nail or glue the template to the board so that it will not move. Take advantage of and use any curve in the wood grain that may correspond to the curve in the frame. Remove the template and cut out the frame with the saw blade set at the appropriate greatest bevel. Cut out only the outboard side of the frame.

Adjust the bevels. After the outboard side of the frame is cut out at the maximum bevel, use the bevel gauge set at the appropriate angle for each station to compare how much the bevel needs to be adjusted for that station. The bevel can be adjusted by plane or belt sand the outboard side of the frame so that it corresponds to the angle of the bevel gauge. The bevel gauge should lay flat against the frame when the correct bevel is made. This is done for each station. For making very large sawn frames, it is necessary to use a large band saw or ship's saw and adjust the bevel at the table while the frame is being cut out.

Fitting the sawn frame. Place the cut-out side of the frame against the hull. If it doesn't seat flat on the planking, put some colored chalk on the planking and rub the frame forward and aft along the strike-up marks. Flip the frame over and belt sand or plane where the chalk marks are till the frame fits tightly against the planking or until the chalk marks the entire outboard side of the frame.

Marking and cutting the inboard side. When the outboard side of the frame fits tightly against the hull planking, mark the inboard side of the frame. This is done by pressing a flexible fairing batten against three or more frames at one side of the new frame and marking where the outboard side of the batten touches the new frame at each of the stations (one-foot intervals). These marks correspond with where ceiling or stringers would intersect the new frame's inboard surface. The marks are joined with a flexible fairing batten and a line is drawn on the side of the frame. This process of finding and marking the inboard side of the new frame is repeated for the other side of the frame. The inboard side of the frame is cut oversized and planed or sanded to the lines marked with the fairing batten on both sides of the frame.

Repeat. This process is repeated for the other section of the sawn frame. Make sure to allow a good overlap, at least enough for three or four through-bolts. Bolt them together, using epoxy in between If the boat is bronze fastened, use bronze through-bolts, the same size as the originals or greater. If iron fastened, use #316 grade stainless steel. Trunnels, or tapered wooden pegs split on the outer side for wedges, can be driven into holes drilled in the frames on angles to join them together.

Fastening the frame. Fit the new frames over where the old frames went so that the old fastener holes are in the middle of the new frames. Mark on the hull where the new frame goes. Wedge the sawn frame or have someone hold it securely from the inside while you drill the fastener hole through the guide hole in the original plank into the new frame from the outside. The correct fastener size for the planking is determined by the thickness of the frame and planking. Use one size bigger diameter screw than was originally used. Drill the fastener hole through the old screw hole in the plank into the new frame with a tapered drill bit of the correct size for the screws you will use. It is better not to use nails for fastening, since hammering may jar loose the adjacent planks. Since it is near impossible to find good galvanized screws any more, if the boat is iron-fastened, use silicone bronze or #316 grade stainless steel or monel screws. The sawn frame can be bedded up or epoxied against the planking, or put in dry tight against the hull. The end-grain and backside (if not the whole frame) should be painted with red lead or other good paint to seal it from absorbing freshwater.

Drill only the hole for the fastener you'll be fastening. Do not drill all the holes at once. Fasten in the frame starting from the bottom and going consecutively toward the top. Make sure that the frame is being held or wedged tightly against the planking from the inside. Slant the fasteners slightly in toward the center of the frame, and use a brace and screwdriver bit of the proper size to fit the head of the screw. Use only flathead wood screws, not sheet metal screws, for fastening the planks to the frames. On large boats, lag bolts can be used. As you tighten the screws you can actually see the planks and hull firming up and going back into shape.

After the last screw is tightened, go back to the garboard and tighten them all again if bedding compound was used, the excess bedding compound will squish out. Then glue in the wood plugs and line up the grain to match the grain of the planks. Use a hammer or wooden mallet to set the wood plugs, being careful not to hit them too hard and crush them. Let the glue harden around the wood plugs. Come back with a sharp, shallow angle, block plane, or soft pad grinder, and fair in the wood plugs so that they are flush with the hull planking. Using a chisel may cause the plug to shear off at an angle deeper than the planking surface. If the countersink hole is too ragged for a wood plug, it can be filled with epoxy.

Remember to bolt the heel of the frame to the adjacent floor timber, bolt the top of the frame to the deck beam, and to screw the sheer clamp to the new frame.

8

BUILDING A STEAM BOX FOR STEAM BENT FRAMES

There are many ways to build a steam generator. The old method is to build a large fire in a fifty-five gallon steel drum under a section of steel pipe partially filled with water. While the water boils, the wood to be bent is placed in the pipe. As the density and pressure increase, the steam is forced to penetrate the wood fibers which become flexible. This is the traditional method of making a steamer. You can use a propane canister to heat a metal can with water inside. The other method is to use an electric steam generator. It is safe, discrete, very portable—only 18 inches long—and can fit in your toolbox whenever you need an on-demand electric hot water heater or steam generator. If a lot of steam bending is to be done, it is well worth constructing this simple device made up of common hardware. The steam generator described here uses a 220-volt hot water heater element. Take the drawing (Figure 12, which lists all parts needed) with you to the plumbing department of any good hardware store, and you will quickly and easily be able to assemble this compact device that will produce an unlimited amount of steam for all your steam-bending projects.

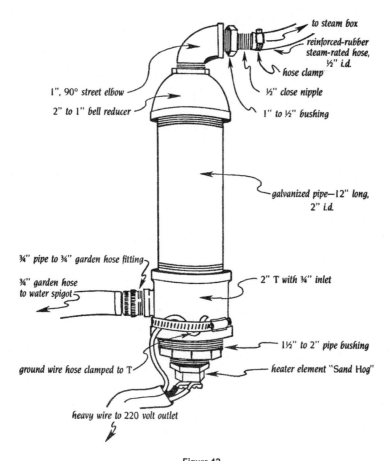

Figure 12
A compact hot water heater—steam generator for steam-bending wood

BUILDING AN ELECTRIC STEAM GENERATOR

• Start by calling some plumbing supply companies in your area until you find a 220-volt, 3500-watt hot water heater element;

they are sometimes called "the Sand Hog." This element will not burn out if operated without a sufficient amount of water running past it.

• Using a good pipe thread sealer to seal all pipe joints, thread the heater element into a 1½-inch to 2-inch pipe bushing.

• Use pipe joint compound again to thread the bushing into a 2-inch T-coupling with a ¾-inch inlet.

• Thread a ¾-inch pipe to garden hose fitting into the ¾-inch inlet of the 2-inch T.

• Into the other end of the 2-inch 'T,' thread a 12-inch-long, 2-inch diameter galvanized steel pipe.

• Onto the other end of the 2-inch pipe, thread a 2-inch to 1-inch bell reducer.

• Into the reducer, thread a 1-inch 90° pipe street elbow.

• Onto the elbow, thread a 1-inch to ½-inch pipe bushing.

• Into the bushing, thread a ½-inch close nipple (or pipe-to-hose-barb for ½-inch pipe to ½-inch hose).

• Then you'll need a good quality, reinforced, steam-rated rubber hose and hose clamp. The length of hose should be long enough to reach from the 1/2-inch nipple to the steam box.

• Buy a length of wire rated to carry 3500 watts at 220 volts. Extension cord wire will not work! Attach the two wires, white to "+", black to "–" to the end of the heater element; the third green wire is held by a hose clamp to the 2-inch T for the ground. Connect the proper electrical plug to fit into the 220-volt outlet to the other end of the wire.

• Thread a ¾-inch garden hose onto the ¾-inch pipe to hose fitting on the 2-inch T.

That completes one of the world's smallest hot water heater steam generators. Plug it in and turn on the water so that it just trickles. Hot water and steam will come out the other end. Do not use PVC fittings anywhere on this device and do not for any reason restrict or stop the flow of steam from the steam generating end of the unit while it is in operation. If water is coming out of the hose end and not steam, turn down the water at the faucet so that it barely trickles out of the hose. Once you find the right amount of water flow, the unit will produce a steady amount of steam until it is shut off. (Figure 12)

Here is a list of plumbing parts you will need:

• 220-volt, 3500-watt hot water heater element called "Sand Hog"

• 1 ½-inch to 2-inch pipe bushing

• 2-inch T with one ¾-inch inlet

• ¾-inch pipe to garden hose fitting

• 12-inch-long 2-inch galvanized steel pipe, threaded both ends

• 2-inch to 1-inch bell reducer

• 1-inch 90° pipe street elbow

• 1-inch to ½-inch pipe bushing

• ½-inch close nipple

• 2 or 3 feet of ½-inch reinforced, steam-rated rubber hose

• Length of electrical wire sufficient to reach from steam box to electrical outlet. Wire should be capable of carrying 3500 watts at 220 volts.

• 220 plug to fit 220-volt electrical outlet

• Hose clamp to fit a 2-inch pipe T

• Hose clamp to fit over a ½-inch hose

• ¾-inch garden hose

• Good pipe joint compound

THE STEAM BOX

You can make a simple steam box out of a length of steel drain pipe, sheet metal chimney pipe, or section of aluminum mast of a large enough diameter and length to contain the wood that will be steamed. In it will be a hole for the ½-inch rubber hose or a ½-inch close nipple and hose to permit the entry of steam. The ends of the steam box will have to be capped with wooden doors or stuffed with rags so the ends can be tightly closed to prevent the loss of steam. You can make steam with a propane tank and burner under a water tank hosed to the steam box or simply by boiling water in a steel drain pipe-steam box big enough to hold the wood to be steamed.

Another type of steam box can be built out of sheets of plywood cut into four, one-foot by eight-foot sides, and fastened together with the help of 1-inch x 1-inch wooden corner supports to form an eight-foot-long box or longer to accommodate pieces to be steamed. Fasten tight-fitting wooden doors with hinges to each end of the box. Fasten a copper tube with holes drilled in it to the inside of the box to form a sprinkler system for the steam. This addition is not totally necessary, as the steam will eventually fill the whole chamber if entered from the middle of the top of the steam box. Drill several small holes in the bottom of the box to allow runoff of excess water. Grates or sticks on the bottom and between layers of wood will help the steam circulate all around the wood as it steams. The steam generator can be fastened to one of the sides of the steam box. (Figure 13)

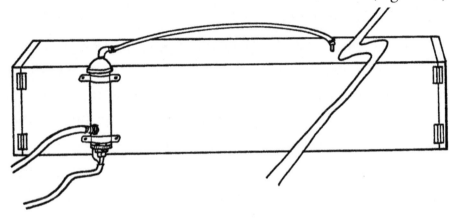

Figure 13

Steam box and steam generator

9
STEAM BENT FRAMES STEP-BY-STEP

Steam Bending on a Jig

Find the amount of bend for the frame by making a template of the inside curve of the hull, where the frame will be placed. Make a bending jig from this template, tightening up the curve a bit (about 25 percent) to allow for the amount that the wood will relax when it is removed from the jig.

Cut the framing wood to the proper dimension, using straight-grained white oak, if possible, steamed in a steam box for approximately one hour per inch of thickness, and clamped to the jig until cool.

Then wedge the steam bent frame into place so that it is tight against the planking and then fasten from the outside.

Steam Bending in Place

If possible, set the steam box close to where the frame will be placed. By using portable stringers or shores and wedges to the deck or carlin, set the freshly steamed frame directly in place and tightly against the hull before it cools. In this way the new steam bent frame when wedged in tightly against the hull will twist and correspond to the bevels of the hull. The new frame does not have to be in the exact same place as the old one or at the same angle.

You have to work very fast because the frame is flexible for only about three minutes after it is taken from the steam box. The frame should be bent by hand (and foot) as soon as it is taken from the steam box. Wear gloves. The areas of maximum bend should have been marked on the frame before steaming. Pre-bending the frame by hand before it is placed against the hull saves time. It is better to over-bend it by hand and straighten the frame out a bit while it is being wedged against the hull.

Sometimes it is necessary to remove a plank at the tightest curve so that clamps can be used through the plank space to assist in seating the frame tightly against the hull. Use wooden pads under the clamp to avoid crushing the wood fibers or splitting the plank by point loading.

The frames should be fastened in from the outside while they are still hot and flexible. This will pull the frames even more tightly against the planking.

Wood for Steam Bending

When selecting wood for steam bending, try to choose straight tight-grained white oak heartwood. Never use sapwood for framing or anywhere else on a wooden boat.

Kiln dried or air dried white oak will do.

Line the end-grain of the frame up parallel to the planking, if possible, so that the fastener does not split the frame by separating the grain. Here, too, the crown of the grain should be facing inboard or away from the planking. Mark "OUTBOARD" on the frame before steaming so that the frame is bent the correct way. (Figure 14)

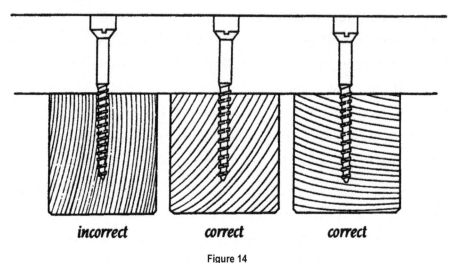

incorrect   correct   correct

Figure 14
Alignment of grain for steam-bent frames

THE STEAM-BENT FRAME STEP-BY-STEP

Making the Bending Jig

• Make a rough template of the hull curve where the steam bent frame will go.

• Draw the curve on four pieces of ¾-inch plywood.

• Using a flexible wooden batten tighten up the curves about 25 percent of those found with the template.

• Draw these curves on the plywood and cut them out with a band saw or a saber saw.

• Fasten the two pieces together with nails, glue, or screws making sure their curves are aligned.

• Fasten the other two pieces together the same way to make the two sides of the bending jig. (Each side should be 1½-inches thick.)

• Securely nail or screw 1 x 2s about 18 inches long to the curved edge of the plywood jig with spaces between big enough to fit clamps.

• This bending jig will be wide enough to bend several frames at a time.

Steam Bending the Frame

• Choose a piece of oak with tight straight grain. Avoid runoff grain that may split when bent. White oak is best for frames.

• It will help to sand off the sharp outboard corner edges after the wood has been cut to the proper dimension. This will prevent the wood from splitting at the edge when being bent or fastened.

• It will help the wood to bend more easily if it is soaked in a salt water solution for at least 24 hours before it is to be steamed. Oil can be added to the solution.

• Have a piece of sheet metal cut to the same dimension or slightly wider than the frame. This will be clamped between the clamp and the steamed frame to prevent the frame from splitting and to insure a fair, smooth curve.

• The rule of thumb is to cook the wood for one hour per inch of thickness, or longer.

• It helps to mark the areas of maximum bend and the word "OUTBOARD" on the frames before they are put into the steam box.

• After the box is filled with steam, place the oak or other suitable wood in the steam box and close the door. Place the wood to be steamed on slats or a grate so that the steam reaches all sides.

• After about an hour, you'll be able to smell the sweet smell of oak cooking. Black tannic water will pour out the drain holes at the bottom of the steamer. Be patient.

• Spray the clamps with WD-40 to make sure they are free. Have the plywood pads ready and place them with the clamps near the bending jig.

• When the wood is ready, open the box. Using heat pads or rags, pull out one steamy frame. Shut the door.

• Immediately bend the frame to the places marked as maximum bend and bring it to the jig already bent. (Use your hands and feet or any way you can to bend the frame as soon as it leaves the box. Don't wait till you get it clamped to the jig as it will be too cool to bend by then. It is okay to over-bend it because it will be easily straightened while you are clamping it onto the jig).

• Clamp it to the jig using the sheet metal and plywood pads under the clamps.

• Leave the frame in the jig till it cools off.

• Bend up the rest of the frames and clamp them to the jig. If room is needed on the jig, wait till the frame is cool, then tie the curve into the frame with a piece of string, or nail a stay lath on both sides, making sure that the frame does not twist along its curve. Lay it flat and if you have to, weight it down so it doesn't twist.

• When the cooled frame is removed from the jig, it will straighten out or relax a bit. Check it against the template you made to see if it is still close to the right curve. If the curve of the hull changes radically in the section that needs to be reframed, it may be necessary to make several bending jigs of the different curves. If the curves are similar, one jig will suffice.

FITTING THE STEAM-BENT FRAME

• Place the steam bent frame in where it will go.

• (Assuming that the old frame was completely removed.) The new frame must cover the fastener holes and its outline marked on the inside of the hull. The curve of the steamed frame should be pretty close to that of the hull.

• Where the heel of the frame touches the keel, mark the angle on the frame. This angle can be marked by using a sliding bevel gauge. If yours is too big to fit into the space, make a handy, mini-bevel gauge by breaking a few inches off the ends of a dull hacksaw blade and using a copper rivet or small nut to bolt through the two holes at the ends (Figure 4)

• Cut the angle at the end of the frame along the mark made using the homemade, mini-bevel gauge and paint the end grain of the frame with red lead, enamel or epoxy. If there is a socket carved into the keel for the butt end of the frame, make sure it is cleaned out and that the bottom of the new frame fits all the way into that socket.

• Screw a cleat (piece of wood) into the side of the keel or floor timber to hold the heel of the frame tightly against the garboard if there is no socket. It may be necessary to drive some shallow angle wooden wedges between the cleat and the heel of the frame in order to seat the frame tightly against the hull. Do not drive it in too hard, don't loosen the garboard.

• This is a "dry run." You are trying to determine if it will work, if you have considered all the procedures involved, if you have all the tools needed to complete the entire job. Make sure that the frame is in the right spot and that you have enough wedges to secure the frame. It is better not to through-bolt frames through the planks as this significantly weakens the frame and gives a pathway for a leak should the fastener corrode. If the frame doesn't fit perfectly against the planking, then it will be necessary to use a method that I call the "Portable Stringer Method."

PORTABLE STRINGER METHOD

• ¾-inch-thick plywood "hangers" are cut out with a band saw or saber saw.

• Screw or clamp hangers to the sides of the adjacent frames beside where the new steam bent frame will go. That is why it is important to remove only one frame at a time and replace that frame before removing the next one. (Figure 15)

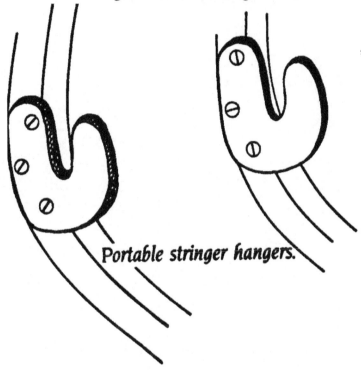

Portable stringer hangers.

Figure 15

• Position the hangers so that they are in the area where there is the most gap between the frame and the hull.

• Use a 1 x 2 oak scrap, a fir 2 x 4, or a piece of steel angle-iron to fit into the 'U' of the hanger that was cut out of ¾-inch plywood. Drive wooden wedges between the new frame and the stringer; force the frame tightly against the hull. Do this in several places to seat the frame. By this method, you will be able to do the entire job of framing by yourself without needing assistance from anyone else. (Figure 16)

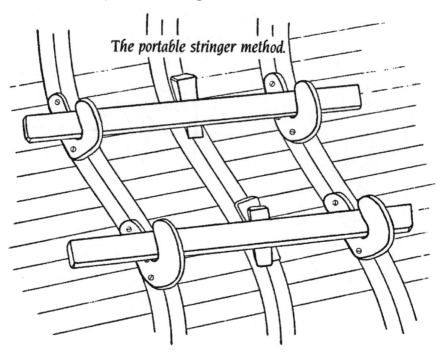

The portable stringer method.

Figure 16

• If the frame is near a bulkhead, screw the hanger to the bulkhead. Shores from the opposite side of the hull, deck, and cabin are also effective in forcing a frame into place.

• If the frame doesn't seat flat on the hull and one side is away from the planking, you may have to grind the backside of the frame until it fits. Use chalk on the hull to mark the high spots on the frame. Grind off the chalk marks or high spots until the frame fits flat against the hull.

• Now that you have checked that the new frame can be tightly

100

pressed and seated flat against the hull and all the stringers and wedges are in place, remove the new frame.

• Make sure that the hull is clean, smooth, and vacuumed. The use of bedding compound or epoxy between frame and planking is optional. If bedding compounds are used, only a very thin coat is needed; otherwise, the frame will not seat tightly against the planking.

• The new frame is ready to install. Place the frame between the two lines so that the screw holes will end up on the frame.

• Install the keel wedges to hold the heel of the frame tightly against the hull.

• Install the portable stringers and the stringer wedges starting at the bottom and working upwards.

• Check to see if you are still on the mark and that the frame is pressed tightly against the hull.

• Use a spade bit or wood bore, drill or clean up the original countersunk hole from outside. If re-drilling the countersunk hole is necessary, you may need to first glue in a wood plug to give the drill a center to start the hole. Mark the drill bit with masking tape or paint to a depth of about ¼ of the thickness of the plank; for soft wood, drill slightly less than a quarter of the plank's thickness.

• It is a good idea to use a screw of a larger size diameter than the original fastener used.

• The length of the screw will be about twice the thickness of the planking. Draw a diagram of the planking and frame to scale to determine the length of the fastener needed. (Figure 17)

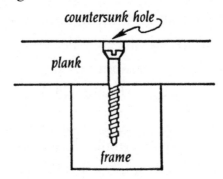

Figure 17
The screw should penetrate about three-fourths of the way through the frame.

• Once again it is better not to use boat nails or square nails. Nailing may impact load the hull too much and loosen the adjacent planks. Use #316 grade stainless steel or monel wood screws if your boat is iron fastened; use silicone bronze screws or copper rivets if your boat is bronze or copper riveted. You can dip the screws in red or white lead, paint, or epoxy to make them slide in easily.

• Start at the garboard, drill the screw hole with a tapered drill bit for the correct size screw you will be using. Mark the drill bit with masking tape or paint a mark on it at the desired depth for the screw.

• *Drill and fasten in one screw at a time,* start at the bottom and work upwards to the sheer plank.

• Use a hand-brace and screwdriver bit of the correct size so that it perfectly fits the slot of the wood screw. Tighten each screw as hard as you can, going inside occasionally to check that the wedges are still in place and that the frame has not moved. The frame should be tight against the hull and you should see the bedding compound squishing out the sides from between the frame and the hull. *Never pre-drill all the screw holes before you start fastening.* The frame will "stretch" as it is fastened, and if the holes are pre-drilled, they will end up in the wrong spot.

• If bedding compound squishes out between frame and plank, clean the excess with paint thinner or alcohol on a rag. (Cooking oil, or vinegar will often dissolve uncured epoxy, bedding compounds, and paint off your skin better than strong solvents which dissolve the protective oils from your skin. White vinegar will remove uncured epoxy resin from your skin or from wood. Working on boats can be hazardous to your body so it is very important to take all the precautions you can to minimize your exposure to dangerous fumes, dusts, and chemicals.)

• Go back and check the screws from the outside to see if you can tighten them up. As the bedding compound squishes out, tighten the screws.

• Wood plugs should be installed the same day because if the end grain around the countersunk hole is allowed to absorb moisture from the damp night air, it can change shape and make it impossible to fit and glue in a new wood plug.

• If you have a plug cutter, cut plugs from scraps of wood of the same type as that of the hull planking. Otherwise, buy some teak or Honduras mahogany plugs. Teak is good for wood plugs, don't use soft Philippine mahogany ones. Dip the plugs in epoxy so that they are covered to a depth about half-way up their sides; also, paint glue around the sides of the plug hole. Insert the plug so that the grain corresponds with the grain of the planking.

• After you fasten the frame, remove the wedges, portable stringers, and hangers and fill with epoxy the screw holes in the sides of the adjacent frames as well as any gaps between the laminations that can't be wedged any tighter.

• Bolt the new frame to the floor timber and deck beam and the sheer clamp.

Always strive to do a good job. Attention to details is often the difference between a job well done and a careless job. Always aim for high quality. The satisfaction you derive from your efforts will be your reward.

THE DECK COVERING-BOARD METHOD OF INSTALLING STEAM-BENT FRAMES

This method is used for sistering if the original frames are broken, not rotten, and if no access can be gotten from the inside. This may be because there are full ceilings (a layer of planking on the inside of the frames), or tanks in the way or built-in interiors that cannot be removed, or if the space is too small to enter from the inside, such as the space in the counter stern of an Alden-designed sailboat.

Remove a plank or two from the outside, usually at the turn of the bilge, so that you can insert a clamp to help clamp the frame to seat tightly against the planking. Usually, there is a covering board or margin board at the outboard edge of the deck. It is the most outboard plank of the deck. The toe rail or bulwarks *may* have to be removed to get the covering board out. Be neat, remove the plugs and screws, and remove the covering board at the nearest joint so that it can be reinstalled later. You may need to cut the covering board with a saber saw, sawzall or router. If there is a sub-deck or plywood deck under this, cut inspection holes in it so that a freshly steamed frame can be slid, still hot and flexible, into the hole and against the inboard side of the planking.

You must weigh this method against the other method of installation from the inside. Put the oak in the steam box and steam it as previously described. It is better, however, to set the steam box up on deck near where frame(s) will need to be installed when they come out, and will not cool off too fast. Make the frame longer than it needs to be so that it will stick out through the deck when you have it in place.

It will help to bevel the outboard bottom edge of the frame so it will not catch on the planking seams. Bevel also the end of the frame that will seat against the keel or in the keel socket. Drive the freshly steamed frame through the hole in the deck with a wood block held on top of the frame using a heavy sledge hammer.

A helper is needed below to guide the steaming hot frame past the stringers and to tell you when the frame is tight up against the keel. He will need a long screwdriver or pry bar or crow bar, C-clamps, and plywood pads to guide the frame past the turn of the bilge and clamp it tightly to the planking with a pad on the outboard side of the plank through the removed planking space.

Then, using a long flexible batten, mark with a pencil the centerline of the new frame on the outside of the hull. Line the center of the frame up with the part that appears through the removed planking hole and the part that sticks through the deck. Drill small inspection holes through the planking along the line you marked to determine if you are on the center of the new frame. If not, plug the holes with tiny dowels whittled out of wood. Plug these with epoxy or wood plugs, and drill another hole till you find the center of the frame. Wedge the heel of the frame, if you can get to it. with a wooden wedge and cleat pushing it against the garboard. If the original frames were socketed into the keel, force the heel of the frame into that socket or carve out a new socket.

Starting at the garboard, drill and fasten the frame as described in the previous chapter. Also, if possible, fasten the frame to the floor timbers, deck beams, and sheer clamp. Then replace the covering board, planking, and toe rails or bulwarks that were removed.

This method of driving the steamed frames through the deck is risky, for if they cool too much, the steam bent frames will refuse to bend and be driven down any farther and may break or split the planking or force the planks away from the other frames. One trick to make the steam bent frame more flexible longer is to add more oil to the steaming process. In Cuba, the shipwrights boil the frames in oil.

If it can be avoided it is usually better not to attempt driving steam bent frames through the covering board and to approach the job from the inside.

Turn-of-the-Bilge Sister Frames

Sometimes it is not possible to sister with full-length frames. If sister frames are needed at the turn of the bilge, try to make these as long as possible: at least four or five planks above and below the weak area. It is always a mistake to install very short frames that only cover the turn of the bilge, as these will make a local hard-spot that may cause the original frames to break somewhere else when the boat is worked.

10
LAMINATED FRAMES

We are still assuming in this chapter that the entire frame has been removed.

CHOOSING THE WOOD

The frames in the bow section of the boat are not very curved and rarely break. If it is necessary to replace these, laminated frames can be bent in cold. However, the frames in the midsection of the vessel and in the counter may have radical double curves, which are much more vulnerable to breaking and rotting. These midsection frames, if needing replacement, should only be removed and replaced one at a time or remove every other frame.

To do a proper job of laminating frames it may be necessary to steam bend each lamination of the laminated frame or use many thin laminations that will bend cold. A good laminated 2 x 2-inch frame can be made up of eight laminated ¼-inch x 2-inch oak sections glued together with a good epoxy. Sometimes ½-inch x 2-inch white oak flooring can be bought in long lengths.

If you use flooring oak for framing, plane or cut off the tongue and groove and belt sand or plane the edges of the strips together so that they are all even. It is a good idea to stack a group that will make one total frame together when you plane and sand so that they will all be the same. Also pass the strips through a planer, jointer or sand them to remove any factory coating that was applied to them.

If you decide to use flooring oak, choose wood that has the straightest grain possible; avoid run-off grain or elliptical-patterned slash grain. If the flooring oak has a bend to it, use this to your advantage, use this bend so it corresponds with the bend of the curve of the hull.

If you are unable to find flooring white oak, or if the frames need to be wider than 2 inches, then you must go to a lumber yard for oak planks of the same thickness as the width of your frames. If the frame is to be 2 inches wide, then the oak board must be 2 inches thick. Here, air-dried white oak is the first choice, and kiln-dried white oak is the second choice. The end grain *must* be sealed with glue. Choose a plank that has straight tight grain for ripping into frame laminations. Set up a guide and rip the oak on a table saw. Sometimes white oak can be purchased directly from a boat builder or a boatyard.

THE LAMINATED FRAME STEP-BY-STEP: MAKING THE TEMPLATE FOR THE STEAM-BENDING JIG

In Chapter 7, read the section on *"Making the Rough Template."*

This will describe how to measure for and make a rough template from the curve of the hull where the new frame will go. Use a tight string as a straight line and measure in from the string to the maximum curve. You will end up transferring these measurements onto a sheet of ¼-inch plywood and cutting out the curve with a saber saw or band saw. This does not need to be a perfect template; just get the rough curve of the new frame. Lay the template on a wooden deck or dock or plywood nailed on a 2 x 4 frame, and trace the curve with chalk.

You will need to over-bend these laminations as you did with the steam bent frame, so tighten the curves up by about 25 percent and re-mark the new curve on the wooden floor. Use a flexible batten to mark the fair curve. Nail or screw wooden blocks to the floor, deck, or plywood base to form the bending jig. If using a dock, wooden wedges can be placed between spaces in the dock boards along the curve. The laminations, once they are steamed, will dry in this bending jig. Make this bending jig wide enough so that all the laminations necessary to make one frame can be held together at the same time to dry. (Figure 18)

STEAMING THE LAMINATED FRAME

• If there are a lot of frames to steam, use a steam generator and steam box, as described in Chapter 8.

• It is advisable to mark the laminations where the area of maximum bend will be so that they can be hand-bent as soon as they are taken from the steam box, before they are placed in the jig.

• Set up the generator with the water just trickling past it, get up the steam pressure, and start cooking the oak.

• After about an hour of steaming, the wonderful smell of fresh oak will fill the air, but don't rush it; it's better to have them come out of the steam box like noodles. Go over the procedure, making sure that you have a towel, heat pad, or gloves, to remove the hot oak noodles. Check the jig to make sure it is well fastened—since there will be a lot of pressure on it—and that you have enough clamps standing by.

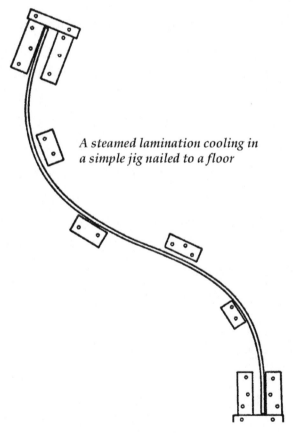

A steamed lamination cooling in a simple jig nailed to a floor

Figure 18

• Okay, remove the first piece of oak.

• Shut the door to the box.

• As soon as you take the oak out of the box start to bend it while you move quickly to the jig. This is necessary, because the wood cools rapidly.

• Place it in the jig.

• Allow it to cool before stacking it together with any other laminations of the same curve.

• If you've ever seen laminated frames before, you've probably seen a poor example of laminated frames. To do a proper job, the laminations should be steam bent. The finished laminated frame, once painted, should look like a solid frame, without spaces between the laminations, without spaces between the frame and hull, and without great goobers of epoxy everywhere.

• Take one of the steam bent laminations once it is dry and stick it against the hull where the frame will go so that it covers the fastener holes. Check to see that the curve is similar to that of the hull and mark the outline of the lamination on the hull with a pencil so that the fastener holes are in the middle of the frame.

• Cut out the "portable stringer hangers" as described. Make a good supply of wedges. Oak is great for wedges but be sure to bevel the top edges so they don't split.

• Now for the dry-run—set the laminations in place, stacked up to the right thickness of the finished frame.

• Fasten the portable stringer hangers to the sides of the adjacent frames beside the frame you are working on. Place these hangers in the areas where the laminated frame is farthest away from the hull. (Figure 19)

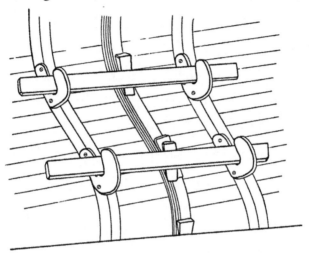

Figure 19

Wooden wedges driven under portable stringers hold laminations tightly together and against the hull.

• Mark the angle between the frame and the keel.

• Nail or screw a cleat to the side of the keel or floor timber and drive wedges between the cleat and the heel of the frame to force the heel tightly against the garboard. If the keel has a socket cut in it for the frame, the laminations must fit into it.

• Work upwards from the garboard setting up the stringers in the hangers and driving in the wedges, making sure that the laminations are all stacked up in line. Sometimes it is necessary to use clamps, wax paper and pads along their sides to keep the laminations lined up straight. Go on setting up the stringers and wedges till the laminations are all held tightly together against the hull.

• If the dry-run is okay, disassemble the pieces, keep the wedges and stringers near where they will be needed.

• Cut out the bevel at the bottom of the frame along the angle marked. Cut and sand them in a stack so they are all the same and will all fit together to form the correct angle.

• Check the planking surface for fairness and smoothness. It may be necessary to soft-pad it smooth and re-mark the lines where the frame will go. Vacuum the area clean.

• After you've vacuumed, set up the fan so you have fresh air.

• It is better to mix and thicken the epoxy outside to cut down on fumes below. Use epoxy thickened to butter-like consistency with colloidal silica or any other thick epoxy that you have thoroughly tested. Mix only enough to spread epoxy on both sides of one lamination at a time, no more than about 10 squirts from a pump to avoid the epoxy from going off before it is used.

• Wear a dust mask when mixing the epoxy and silica, and gloves when working with epoxy.

• Make sure that the epoxy is mixed in the right proportions. Use *slow catalyst.*

• Cut little V's in a plastic spreader to leave just the right amount of epoxy on the back and front of the frame laminations. Cut it to the same width as the frame. This will spread a neat layer of epoxy on the laminations. (Figure 20)

• Spread the epoxy on the planking between the marks you made for the frame. This will need to be thicker to fill any irregularities in the surface.

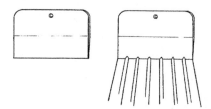

Figure 20
A plastic spreader with notches cut in it for neat glue lines

• The laminations must be dry. Coat the outboard side of the first lamination and stick it in place. If it goes up under the sheer clamp or shelf, put epoxy on the end grain and where it will be hard to spread epoxy when this first lamination is in place. Also, cover the end grain at the bottom of the frame lamination.

• Spread epoxy on the inboard side of the first lamination once it is in place.

• Spread epoxy on the outboard side of the second one; place it on the first one.

• Do this with all of the laminations, spreading epoxy on both sides of each lamination (except for the inboard surface of the last one) and seal all end-grain.

• Line the laminations up in a neat stack.

• Set up the portable stringers.

• Set the heel wedges.

• Starting at the bottom, set the wedges up behind the portable stringers.

• Use plywood pads and clamps at the sides of the laminations to keep them in a neat stack. Use wax paper so the pads don't stick to the epoxy.

• Make sure that the laminations are tight against each other and against the hull and that there are no spaces between them.

• Wipe off any excess epoxy and take off your gloves.

• Go outside. If the plug holes are too ragged, they may need to be re-drilled with a wood bore drill bit. They shouldn't be any deeper than 1/4 the thickness of the planking, a little less for softwood like cedar.

• Fasten in the frame starting from the bottom, use a tapered drill bit of the proper size for the screws and work consecutively upwards to the sheer plank. Screw the sheer clamp to the new laminated frame.

• Leave stringers and wedges till frame laminations set up and epoxy is hard and dry.

• Remove the wedges, portable stringers, and hangers from the sides of the frames and fill the old screw holes from the hanger fasteners with epoxy. When bolting the laminated frame to a floor timber or deck beam, use a block of wood laid against the side of the laminated frame to prevent it from splitting or separating the laminates; drill through and fasten the block to the side of the frame and bolt all three parts together.

ALTERNATIVE METHODS OF LAMINATING FRAMES

Sometimes it is necessary to remove a plank in the area where the maximum bend occurs to allow a clamp to be used from the outside to help clamp the laminations together. Choose a plank at the turn of the bilge or hardest bend for removal, one that has already pulled away from the frames or needs seam repair.

The dry run will tell you if it is possible to wedge the laminations together tightly enough from the inside only or if plank removal will be necessary. Use 2 x 4 shores and wedges from the inside under deck beams, behind stringers and behind carlins to hold the laminations together and tightly against the hull. When driving wedges and shores do not overload the hull or deck. Shores should be used at 90° to the objects they are shoring. *Be careful:* shores and wedges are under tremendous loads.

Another method can be used to pre-bend and glue laminated frames. Here an accurate bending jig is made. In this method, follow the procedure for making a bending jig as described in the section on steam bent frames, however, do *not* allow for over-bending when making the jig. Make an accurate template of the curve at the frame and the outboard surface of the laminated frame in the jig should follow this curve closely. Glue the laminations and clamp to the jig.

After the glue has dried, the frames can be removed from the jig, and the excess glue sanded from their edges. Mark the bevels on the sides of the frame, and belt-sand, hand or power-plane to the correct bevels. The bevels will be greater at the ends of the boat than in the midship area. If there is a radical bevel and it is necessary to remove a lot of wood from the outboard and inboard sides of the frame, allowance must be made by increasing the number of laminations in the frame and there-by making the frame thicker.

Bevel the inboard surface also to accommodate for string-ers or ceilings. Beveling is not necessary in frames laminated in place because the laminations will twist to conform to the hull bevels if adequate pressure can be exerted on them. The very best method of laminating frames is to do them in place and not on a bending jig.

SISTER FRAMING WITH LAMINATED FRAMES

Use sister frames between broken frames or if part of the frame is rotten and the rotten section is replaced. A full-length sister frame that's near a damaged frame will retain the continuity lost by cutting and replacing the deteriorated part of the original frame. Sister frames should be as long as possible, at least five plank spaces both above and below the damaged area.

Mark the hull from the inside where the new sister frame will go. This is done by laying the first lamination between the frames where it is needed so that it lays flat against the planking. It does not matter if the frame is put in on a slant to the rest of the frames, if that is what it takes to have it lay flat against the hull.

In the old days, it was thought that a sister frame needed to lay up close to the frame it sistered. Sometimes a steam bent sister frame was through-bolted through the frame it sistered. This practice is now discouraged as it weakens both frames to through-bolt them and if steel bolts are used, the frames may become iron-sick and eventually rot out again. Also, dirt and water get trapped between the closely-spaced frames. It is better to place the sister frame away from the frame it sisters. Spacing the fasteners too closely together in the plank destroys the continuity of the strength of the planking grain. Mark the first lamination on the hull where the sister frame will go. Now take a small drill bit and drill holes in the planks *from the inside,* two holes to a plank, top and bottom edge, diagonally opposite sides of the frame, to mark the fastener. (Figure 21)

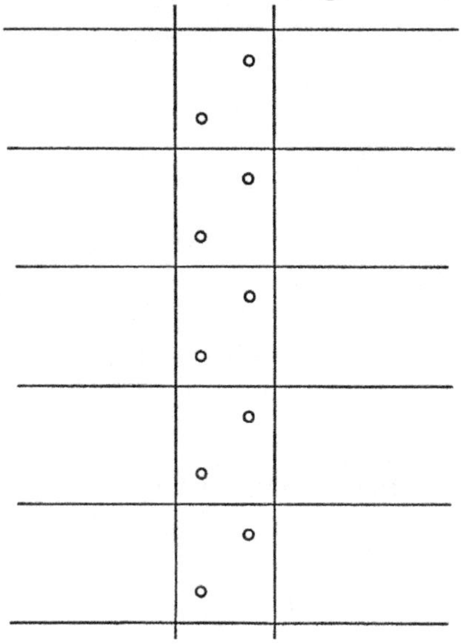

Figure 21
Small holes drilled from the inside with a tapered bit

Set up the portable stringers as described in the previous section on laminated frames. Spread thickened epoxy on the inboard side of the hull and between the laminations and fasten the sister frames with wood screws from the outside.

11

REPLACING TRADITIONAL CARVEL PLANKING

PLANKING THEORY

On the following pages you will find a step-by-step account of the process of replacing a single plank or "shutter or whiskey plank." But first you must understand a few subtle concepts.

Template making—transiting from the 2nd to the 3rd dimension

You all know that when trying to cut a cone out of a piece of paper, you cannot simply cut out a long rectangle and bend it into the shape of a cone. No matter how hard you try, the two-dimensional flat rectangle cannot be made into a three- dimensional cone (Figure 22). There is, however, one and only one two-dimensional shape, that when cut out and bent will form the exact shape of the three-dimensional cone. (Figure 23)

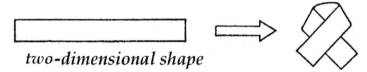

two-dimensional shape

three-dimensional shape is not a cone

Figure 22

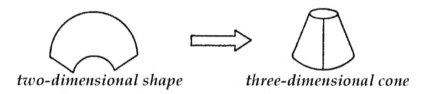

two-dimensional shape　　　　*three-dimensional cone*

Figure 23

Now that you understand this concept, you'll also under-stand why a straight plank cannot be made to fit into an opening in a three-dimensional, curved, and rounded hull. (Figure 24)

There is, however, one and only one two-dimensionally shaped plank that will fit into the three-dimensional opening in the hull (Figure 25). No tape measure in the world will be able to tell you the correct shape of that plank. That is why we have to make a precisely accurate template.

The important consideration when fitting planks is that the inboard or inside edges of the planks must touch each other. The outside or outboard edges will have caulking bevels, so their fit is not as critical. (Figure 26)

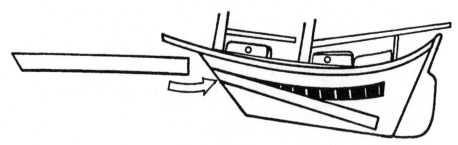

Figure 24
Straight plank will not fit into hull

Figure 25
Perfect fit!

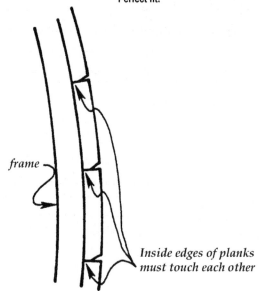

frame

*Inside edges of planks
must touch each other*

Figure 26

PLANKING OVERVIEW

When replacing a "shutter plank"—a single carvel plank, remove the damaged one, make butt blocks and fasten them. Fair the edges of the adjacent planks with a sanding board to smooth out any irregularities or bumps that will interfere with fitting in the new plank. Be careful not to round out or alter the caulking bevel if there is one. Prep the frames, fill fastener holes, and check the frames for fairness with a flexible batten so that they are ready to accept the new plank. Mark the location of the frames on the planks above and below the new plank and put an "X" where the new fasteners should go. Paint the edges of the adjacent planks so any tight spots will leave a paint mark on the new plank while it is fitted.

Then make a form-fitting spiling template so that it fits into the space where the old plank was without touching the edges of the adjacent planks. Glue strips of template stock to the edges of the spiling template to touch the adjacent plank edges. Write WRONG SIDE on the outboard side. Remove the spiling template. The spiling template should not be so tight that it has to be pried out. It should come in and out easily without having to bend it. If it is too tight, then the plank will be too hard to get in. *Flip over the spiling template to the opposite side,* (a step that if omitted, will cause the plank to fit poorly), write THIS SIDE UP on it. Then trace the outline of the spiling template onto the INBOARD side of the board that will be the new plank. Set a circular saw for the appropriate greatest bevel.

Cut out and fit the plank. Plane the tight spots so that the plank fits tightly along the inboard edge of the neighboring planks and tightly against the frames. Remove the plank, mark the caulking bevel on the outboard edges (if the adjacent planks have no caulking bevels) and plane caulking bevel. Seal the end grain with paint. Fasten one end. Wedge the plank in all the way against the frames and fasten to the frames. Through-bolt the end to the butt blocks with countersunk carriage bolts or flat-head machine bolts. Drive cotton into the caulking seam and paint the cotton immediately with red lead, bottom paint or good thick enamel paint. Fair the plank in with a soft pad grinder or hand plane and fairing board with coarse sand paper. Blow the seams clean with air and "pay" with seam compound.

Edge Set

Another important consideration about the spiling template is when fitting it into the removed plank opening be very careful not to let it bend up or down at all. It must be cut out in the appropriate shape so that it fits into the opening and is about ½ inch smaller than the opening on all sides. It cannot touch the sides of the adjacent planks anywhere because, if it does, this will cause the spiling template to bend. Any bend that the template has to make will mean that the new plank will have to bend up or down to fit into the hole. Use 1/8th-inch doorskin for the template. Join two or three of these together to simulate the curve of the new plank. Fasten them together securely and mark the ends so you can make sure they haven't moved when the spiling template is removed. Bending of the template or plank to get it to move up or down to fit into the hole is called "edge set". Edge setting is used in new boat construction. When installing new planks, they are forced up or down and wedged in tight against each other with clamps. But you cannot and should not edge set when installing shutter planks.

Make sure, also, to drive the nails that hold the spiling template onto the frames square to the template. If you drive them in at an angle, the template will bend up or down. Leave the heads sticking up so you can pull them out after the template is finished.

Crown Out

Before you nail the template to the board that will be the new plank, belt-sand the end grain of the board to determine the direction of the cup of the grain. You want the shortest grain possible, but if there is any crown to it, the crown must face OUT (away from the template and the frames) when the plank is fastened in. (Figure 27)

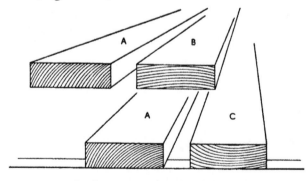

Figure 27

The type and direction of wood grain for planking. The short, quarter-sawn grain in plank A is much more stable than the long grain in plank B. Plank A will not swell as much as plank B. Always "crown up" as in A and B. Never crown down as in C.

125

PLANKING SURVEY

You've surveyed the wooden boat and for one reason or another you've determined that a new plank or planks are necessary. Maybe worms have bored into the seams or iron fasteners have softened and deteriorated the wood. Careless caulking could have ruined the seams or maybe there is a soft butt end. The plank could be split or cracked from collision, severe dry out or over-fastening. It could be chafed at the waterline from rubbing on a pile or against a dock, and the fasteners are too close to the surface, or the plank too thin from wear. Short planks will need to be replaced with long planks, and planks replaced if butts are too close together.

Whatever the reason, you've decided to replace the plank. If a large area needs to be re-planked, *do not remove all the planks at once*, unless new frames need to be inserted from the outside. Replace only one plank at a time. If replacing a large area of planking that had to be removed all at once, the space will have to be divided up into appropriately spaced plank-width sections by nailing fairing battens to the frames to establish where the planks will go and spiling to the edge of these battens. If too many planks are removed at a time, you can compromise the shape and structure of the hull.

PLANNING THE PLANK

Space the butts so there are at least five frames between butts on adjacent planks. It is usually necessary to remove the paint from the area to find the butts. *Long planks are always better than short planks.* Make new planks as long as possible. The longer they are, the more securely they will be fastened. Short planks weaken the structure of the vessel and are harder to secure. It is not good practice to replace a section of planking shorter than 10 feet in length where possible.

Look closely from the inside for butt blocks on the nearby planks. If the plank is being taken out from one existing butt block to the other existing butt block—are the original butt blocks still good? Usually they need to be replaced as well. Are the ends of the planks on either side of the plank you are replacing still good? Or are they soft, split, or iron-sick? If the ends of adjacent planks are bad, the new plank will have to extend farther so that the ends of the other planks can be cut back to better wood. If the plank is butted on a frame, as in workboat construction, then the ends will need to be cut back farther and proper butt blocks installed or if the frames are wide enough, cut the adjacent plank back to the middle of the next frame.

If you can't decide if the plank is bad enough to replace and it is soft at one end, remember that soft wood lets water get to the fasteners and the fasteners will corrode; this corrosion will also cause rapid deterioration in plank and frame. Rot or iron-sickness in a plank will spread to the frame, stem, or deadwood to which it is fastened.

There is a lot to consider. How will you remove the old plank? How will you put in the new one? What kind of wood will you use? How much will the new plank swell? Are the frames strong enough to hold fasteners?

12

PLANKING STEP BY STEP

This chapter contains a step-by-step description of the process of removing a damaged plank, installing butt blocks, making a spiling template, selecting the wood, taking off bevels, and cutting, fitting the shutter plank, and fastening the new plank.

REMOVING THE PLANK

• Decide where the butts will be. There should be four or five frames between one butt and the next on the planks above or below the one you are replacing. The butts should be in a place where they can be reached from the inside. Mark the end cut-off line with a square. Nail up a router guide. (Figure 28)

• Make the router guide out of a 1-inch x 2-inch wooden batten nailed or screwed onto the hull, square to the plank, so that it doesn't move, but so that it can be removed later when the routing is completed. Nail or screw a top stop and bottom stop to the hull as well.

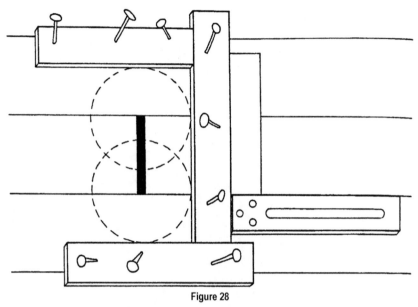

Figure 28

A router and a guide with stops are used to make the end cut on the plank that is being replaced.

• Route through the end of the plank making about 1/4-inch-deep passes, each one deeper than the last, until the plank is cut through. Be careful not to route into the seam of the plank above or below or through the plank and into the frame.

• Do the same for the other end, unless the plank ends on a stem, deadwood, or transom.

• With a circular saw, rip through the middle of the plank from butt to butt. Be careful to set the saw blade so that it is the exact same depth as the thickness of the plank. Wear goggles and a dust mask; there will be a lot of bottom paint dust. (Figure 29)

• For thick hardwood planks that are difficult to break out without excessive prying and beating which may damage or loosen adjacent planks and frames, use a sawzall or sabersaw to cut criss-cross through the planks. *Be careful not to cut into the frames.* Break out the pieces with a screwdriver or pry bar and heavy hammer. Be careful not to hurt the seams of the adjacent planks. (Figure 30)

Figure 29

Rip the plank down the middle with a circular saw set for the depth of the planking thickness

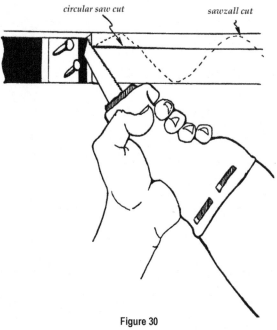

Figure 30
Use a sawzall to cut the plank. Be careful not to cut into the frames.

PREPPING THE FRAMES

Remove the fasteners. If screws, use a screwdriver, brace and bit, or vise grip. If nails, hammer them in a little first to break their hold on the wood, then pull them out with a crow bar or a steel-handled hammer and a block of wood. If they are iron nails and cannot be removed without damaging the frame, break the nail off or grind flush with the surface of the frame, counter-sink them a bit and fill over the countersunk broken-off nail with epoxy.

After the fasteners are removed from the frames, whittle tapered plugs and glue them into the fastener holes in the frames.

Cut off and fair the plugs that were glued into the old fastener holes in the frames after the glue is dry and fill any cracks or cavities in the frames with thickened epoxy.

MARK THE FRAMES AND BUTT BLOCKS

Mark on the plank above and below where the frames and butt blocks are and where new fasteners should be placed so they will not be in the same old fastener holes. (Figure 31)

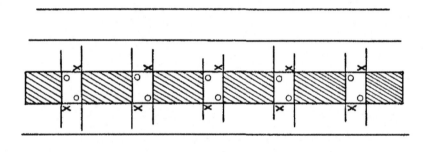

Figure 31
On adjacent planks, draw lines to show the frames and mark X's to indicate the location of the fasteners in the new plank.

PREP THE EDGES OF THE ADJACENT PLANKS

With a straightedge or fairing batten, check the plank edges and straighten out any radical dips that may cause problems when fitting in the new plank. Do not try to make the curves straight, just fair or smooth them out. Use a hand plane, or sanding board made out of a long thin piece of ¼-inch plywood with 60- or 80-grit sandpaper contact cemented onto it to smooth out the edges of the adjacent planks. Clean and sand the frames smooth. Cleaning and fairing the adjacent plank edges will save time later and aid in accurately fitting a new plank. Lay a flexible batten over at least four or five frames to make sure they all are on the same plane and will touch the back of the new plank. Shim any frame shy of the batten or plane or chisel any frame that sticks out too far.

Clean the frames: scrape off the dirt or mud.

Paint with red lead or any good thick enamel paint. Paint the frames well and paint the plank edges with a thin coat. If you are unable to find red lead, use any good enamel paint. *Seal especially the end grain at the butts of the adjacent planks.* The paint will mark the tight spots when fitting the new plank. It is like using chalk to mark the tight spots. The paint should be applied in a thin coat to the adjacent plank edges only, *not to the new plank.* Avoid getting lumps or dirt in the paint that may bind or stop the new plank from seating in all the way.

BUTT BLOCKS

Terminate new planks on bedded and well-fastened butt blocks. The only exception being on very heavily constructed workboats with massive double-sawn frames where ceilings or other permanent installations (tanks, machinery) make the use of butt blocks impractical or impossible. Through-bolt butt blocks.

Making the Butt Block

From inside, measure the size of the butt block needed. (Figure 33)

133

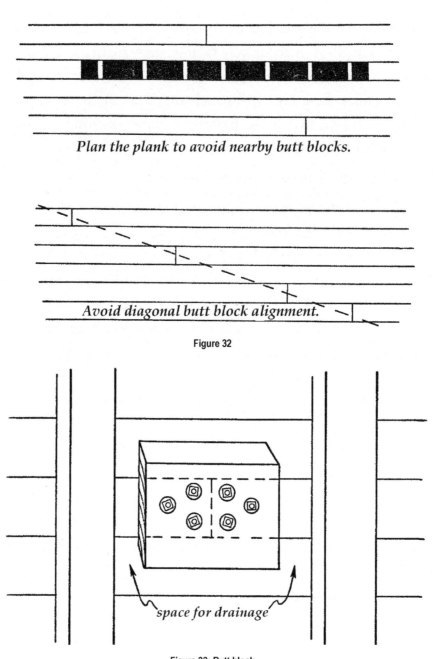

Plan the plank to avoid nearby butt blocks.

Avoid diagonal butt block alignment.

Figure 32

space for drainage

Figure 33: Butt block

The crown of the grain, if there is one, should be facing away from the planking or toward the inside of the boat. The top edge of the butt block is beveled so water will not get trapped behind or on top of it (Figure 34). If frames are not consistently spaced or are closely spaced, the butt blocks should not be closer than five feet to those in adjacent planks. Butt blocks should be placed so that three or more do not form a diagonal line. (Figure 32)

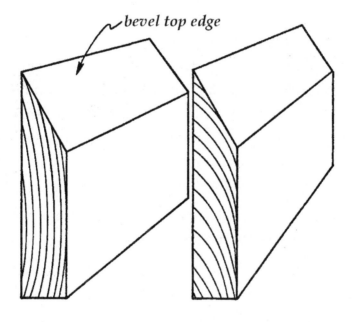

Figure 34

Butt blocks should be at least as thick as the planking and have about one-and-a-half or two inches of overlap on the plank above and below. The fasteners through the butt blocks should be arranged so that two or more do not occur on the same grain line to avoid splitting the butt block or the plank. Butt blocks should be shaped to fit exactly the shape of the planking to which they are fastened. It will be necessary to make a template of the outboard side of the frames and shape the butt block to correspond with that curve. If this is not done, the plank ends or the butt blocks may split. This also causes unfairness at the plank ends and a greater possibility of a leaking butt block. The crown of the grain of a butt block should face away from the planking.

Butt blocks should be as long as possible, but should not extend from frame to frame. There should be space for drainage at either end between the ends of the butt blocks and the frames. Butt blocks should be beveled on the top edge to encourage efficient drainage of fresh water if deck leaks should occur. *The butt block should be well-painted on all sides, especially the outboard side and the end grain and well-bedded.*

Do not use plywood for butt blocks because plywood is very susceptible to rot and delamination.

Bed and securely fasten butt blocks with at least three through- bolts per plank. On planking 3 to 4 inches wide, use three fasteners per plank on each butt block. On planking 4 to 6 inches in width, use five fasteners, and on planking 8 to 10 inches wide, use six fasteners per plank on each butt block. It is best to through-bolt butt blocks with carriage bolts or flat- head machine bolts. Avoid all-thread, or bolts that are threaded all the way up to their heads, or bolts that have expanded threads. (See Chapter 15 "Refastening" for fastening butt blocks.) Quarter-inch diameter bolts are too weak to use for fastening butt blocks except on very small vessels.

Make the butt block out of the wood you are using for planking or framing or hardwood that will resist splitting. White oak, teak, Honduras mahogany, dense or long leaf yellow pine, fir, ipe, or cypress are all good for butt blocks.

Hold the butt block up to the planking. If it rocks or if the top and bottom edges touch and the middle is away from the hull, then it will have to be planed or sanded down so that it lays flat. Make a template of the curve of the hull and shape that butt block to fit that curve. Chalk will help mark the tight spot if it is rubbed on the planking and the butt block moved back and forth over it. Keep marking the high spots and planing them down until the butt block fits flat on the hull. Mark on the inboard side of the planking where the butt block will go.

Mark the place where the new plank will fit on the outboard side of the butt block from the outside.

Put bedding compound on the outboard side of the butt block except where the butt end of the new plank will go.

Seal the end grain of the butt block with paint and paint the whole butt block.

Wet patch (plastic roofing tar or roofing cement) can be used as bedding compound for the butt block or you can use polysulphide bedding compound or Dolphinite.

If the boat is iron fastened, use series #316 stainless steel or galvanized iron carriage bolts coated in epoxy or zinc chromate paint. If bronze or copper fastened, use silicon bronze carriage bolts. For thin planking (under 1 inch), use 5/16-inch carriage bolts. For thicker planking use 3/8-inch or 7/16-inch carriage bolts.

Fasten in the butt block by drilling a countersunk hole for the head of the carriage bolt or flat-head machine bolt. It should be deep enough to permit a wood plug to be well glued over the fastener's head. The plug should be countersunk below the surface about 1/4 of the thickness of the plank or deep enough to securely glue a plug. Mark the drill bit with masking tape or paint as a depth gauge. Use a spade or wood bore bit.

Drill the holes for the butt block bolts in the middle of the countersunk hole. You may be able to fit a C-clamp from the outside through the plank hole to hold the butt block in place while you are drilling it. Use pads under the clamp to protect the plank and butt block.

After you drill the first hole through the plank and butt block, put in the first bolt. Set it into the countersunk hole with a punch and a hammer. Go inside and fasten the flat washer and nut onto the bolt. Tighten up the nut with a socket and ratchet. Make sure that the butt block has not moved. Drill and install the rest of the bolts and remove the C-clamp. Tighten the nuts again after the bedding compound squishes. Don't over tighten these bolts, just get them snug. Watch the bedding compound squish from behind the butt block; and snug them up again.

From outside with thinner or a putty knife, wipe off any bedding compound from around the butt block where the end

of the new plank will go. (Figure 35)

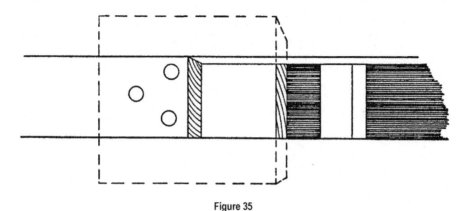

Figure 35

Fasten butt blocks before fitting and marking the spiling batten.

MAKE THE FORM-FITTING SPILING TEMPLATE

Rip a 4 foot x 8 foot piece of ⅛ inch doorskin plywood into the appropriate width that will fit into the planking space without touching the edges of the adjacent planks—so that there is about ½-inch space between the top and bottom edges and ends.

Where the planking space curves or where it exceeds the length of the spiling template, glue and staple two or more pieces of doorskin together securely using generous overlaps and mark the ends to make sure they don't separate or move. Use contact cement or strong "Barge" cement and staples or hot glue and staples.

If the spiling template should touch the adjacent plank edges or ends, plane it down.

FASTEN THE SPILING TEMPLATE

Without allowing the template to bend up or down, fasten it to each of the frames with nails driven into the middle of the template, square to the frames. If the nails are driven in at an angle, the template will bend. If the template is allowed to bend, the plank will have to bend to fit in. Be careful when making the template. Take your time.

• The ends of the doorskin spiling template should not touch the butt ends of the adjacent planks. (Figure 36)

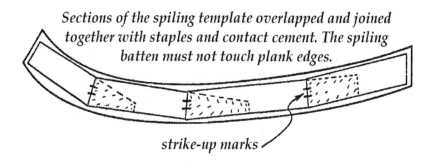

Sections of the spiling template overlapped and joined together with staples and contact cement. The spiling batten must not touch plank edges.

strike-up marks

Figure 36

• Amend the template

• Rip the doorskin into straight 1-inch wide strips on a table saw.

• Starting with the top edge of the spiling template, press the doorskin strip against the lower edge of the adjacent upper plank and with a pencil, mark where the lower edge of the doorskin strip lies against the spiling template. Mark the ends. (Figure 37)

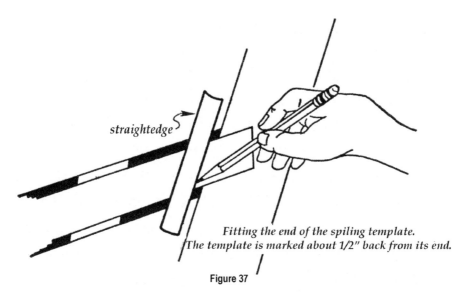

straightedge

Fitting the end of the spiling template.
The template is marked about 1/2" back from its end.

Figure 37

Remove the 1-inch doorskin strip and spread contact cement on the spiling template from the top edge to the pencil line and on the back side of the 1 inch strip. When the contact cement gets sticky, apply a second layer of contact cement. (hot glue can also be used)

When the contact cement feels dry but sticky to the touch, press the 1 inch strip of doorskin against the spiling template so that the upper edge of the strip touches against the lower edge of the upper adjacent plank. There should be no space between the strip and the plank edge.

A few well-placed staples will keep the doorskin from moving on the spiling template.

Repeat this along the lower edge of the template and on the butt ends. (Figure 38)

View the template from the inside of the boat if possible

and look for any light space between the template and plank edge; you should see a thin line of light smaller than a pencil line. Insert a piece of cardboard or paper in any bigger gaps observed from the inside to mark where the template needs to be corrected from the outside by gluing on additional strips or moving the strip up or down to eliminate the gap.

Before removing the template, write "**WRONG SIDE**" on the template. Also mark **TOP, BOTTOM, FWD** and **AFT**.

Check the template, then pull out the nails securing it to the frames. Start at one end and carefully remove the template. The template should come out without binding on the adjacent edges of the planks and without edge setting.

Where the template is too tight to remove, pry it out and sand or plane it. Paint smears will mark the tight spots. Check that it fits back in without binding.

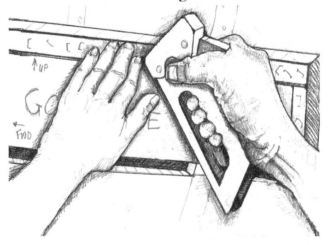

Figure 38
Amending the Template: Strips of doorskin are glued and stapled to spiling template so they touch the edges of the adjacent planks and butts.

FLIP OVER THE TEMPLATE

This is the most important and most overlooked procedure in making well-fit planks.

Importance of Turning Over the Spiling Template

Up to this point, all spiling methods are pretty much the same. Some people use the block, some use a marking stick, some use dividers. However, if the original marks are not transferred to the reverse side of the template there will be a huge inaccuracy in the fitting of the inside edges of the new plank. The greater the difference in thickness between the template and the planking, the greater the inaccuracy will be.

We are using the "FORM-FITTING TEMPLATE METHOD," where the template actually duplicates the shape of the new plank. Visualize what we have done so far. We altered and marked the OUTBOARD face of the template, but we want to mark the INBOARD face of the new plank so that it fits tightly on the INBOARD edges of the adjacent planks. Therefore we MUST flip the spiling template over and use the INBOARD face of the template to trace onto the INBOARD side of the wood to be used for the new plank. *This is the hidden and most forgotten trick to making good templates*. If you have ever watched someone putting in a plank and they had to force the plank up or down to get it to fit into the planking hole, they had not reversed the template. *The plank should be the exact two-dimension shape that, once bent around the curve of the hull, will fit perfectly into the planking hole; it will not need to be*

forced up or down. (Remember the paper cone at the beginning of Chapter 11.)

Forcing a plank up or down to make it fit is called "edge set" and should be avoided. It loads the fasteners, can cause a lightly built boat to hog or change shape, and the plank always wants to spring back out when the hull works or flexes. An edge set plank moves differently than the other planks. An edge-set plank twists away from the frames and is more difficult to seat flat on the frames. The bevel or angle of its edges are not the same as those of the adjacent planks. The caulking seam may be loose in some spots and tight in others. *A properly-spiled plank will need no edge set whatsoever.*

SELECTING WOOD FOR PLANKING

• Belt sand the end grain of the board you have chosen for the new plank so that you can see the grain of the wood.

• The wood should be of straight grain and when looking at the end-grain it should have short quarter-sawn grain if possible. Since wood expands along its grain, a board with long end-grain will swell more in width. (Figures 39 and 40)

• A plank should be selected that has grain like board A. It will have long straight parallel, closely-spaced grain without oval or circular patterns or runoff grain that leave the edge of the board at an angle that may cause the board to spring or bend after it is cut because of locked-in tension. (Figure 41)

• Inspect the wood carefully for tiny holes that indicate the presence of termites or other boring insects.

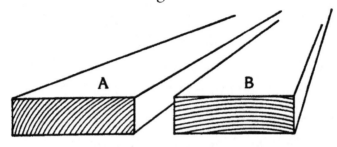

Figure 39

A is a good grain for planking. It will not swell and shrink in width as much as B. The grain in plank B will cup, swell and shrink in width more than plank A.

Figure 40

Wide planks will swell and shrink more than narrow planks.

Clear vertical pin grain; the grain is straight and very close together. This is good grain for planking.

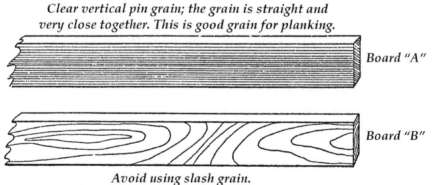

Board "A"

Board "B"

Avoid using slash grain.
This grain may split or lift when the plank is being bent.

Figure 41

• Avoid using sapwood. This can be identified because it is usually found near the edge of the plank. It is also a different color from the rest of the wood; it may be yellowish or greyish. Check both sides of the board for sapwood and if discoloration is found within the wood, avoid including that part of the board in the new plank.

• It is generally a good idea to use the same wood as the boat was originally planked with, unless it was proven that this wood had particularly bad characteristics.

If you choose to plank with mahogany, use Honduras or Cuban mahogany (don't use mahogany for planking if using galvanized nails or screws, mahogany develops a reaction to ferrous metals and will deteriorate around the fastener). Avoid very soft Philippine or Lauann mahogany. If using fir, use Douglas fir. If using oak, use white oak. If pine, use long leaf yellow pine, Dade County pine, or dense Southern pine.

Use Port Orford cedar, Northern, Alaskan white, or yellow cedar. Apitong, cypress, and irokayo are also excellent for planking. When God told Noah to go build an ark, he told him to use cypress. *Tidewater cypress is one of the best woods for planking, it is flexible for bending, easy to plane and work, shipworms won't eat it, it is rot and termite resistant, it absorbs lots of water and swells up very tight.* Shop around and choose your wood carefully. Use recycled wood if possible. Many growth rings are better than fewer, 7 per inch. Air-dried wood is always better than kiln-dried wood. Air-dried wood is stronger and will absorb less water. Never use green wood or wood that hasn't been aged or cured for planking; the rule of thumb is one year per inch of thickness for air-drying. Choose flitches or wide boards, wide enough for the curve of the plank. Test the width by laying the template on the board and make sure the board is wide enough and has no sapwood or run-off grain

Another factor in choosing wood for planking is that local, indigenous wood best suits the conditions of the area where it was grown. Oak, cedar, and fir are fine for planking boats that will always live in the climate where this wood grows, but once in the tropics, these cooler climate woods may rot quickly and become infested with termites and toredos. Woods such as cypress, long leaf yellow pine, Southern pine, apitong, teak, spotted gum wood, teak, ipe and kauri are more suitable for planking boats that will live in tropical waters. Cypress being the best.

Teak is a very unique wood. It is very dense, has a strong distinctive odor, long grain, and changes in color when first cut from light green and pink to a darker, golden honey brown color as it rapidly oxidizes. Teak does not behave in the same manner as other woods. Because it contains such a high percentage of oil, it absorbs almost no water. Most woods expand or swell in the winter when it is cold and damp and contract or shrink in the summer when it is hot and dry. Teak behaves totally opposite. In the winter, when it is cold, teak contracts or shrinks (like metals or other solid materials). In the summer when it is hot, teak expands or swells. Teak is not affected by moisture as much as by temperature. For this reason, teak, a tropically-grown wood, is ideal for use in hot tropical climates and warm waters, where its joints will remain tight. Keeping teak joints and seams watertight in colder climates may be more difficult as the teak contracts and shrinks dimensionally.

Check the thickness of the plank above and below the one that you are replacing to make sure it has a constant thickness. The wood in the new plank will have to be the maximum thickness found.

If the planks are at the turn of the bilge, they may have to have their inboard surface hollowed out to allow them to seat flat on the frames without rocking. Stick a straight piece of wood against the frame and see whether it rocks or lays flat. If it rocks, take a piece of doorskin, hold it alongside the frame, and mark the curve on it. The new plank will need to be hollowed by this amount to fit tightly on this frame. Check a few frames to see if this curve is the same. If not, the plank will need to be hollowed differently for every frame. The new plank will need to be thicker by the amount of the greatest curve found at the frame so that when the inboard side is hollowed, the outboard side of the plank will be at the same level as the adjacent planks. If it is not hollowed, the new plank may split when it is fastened in or it may pull or loosen its fasteners. Sometimes it is easier to grind the frame flat than to hollow out the back of the plank.

The end-grain of the plank should have CROWN away from the template. You will be marking the inboard side of the plank. Write INBOARD on the inboard side of the new plank. (Figure 42)

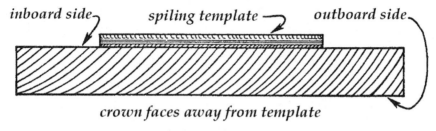

inboard side   *spiling template*   *outboard side*

crown faces away from template

Figure 42

TRANSFERRING THE SHAPE OF THE SPILING TEMPLATE ONTO THE PLANK

Check the strike-up marks to see if they still line up where the sections of template are joined together.

Support the board on saw horses. With "WRONG SIDE" facing **down,** place the template on the INBOARD SIDE of the board that will be the new plank. Check again to make sure the grain of the board has its cup facing down or away from the spiling template. Write the word GOOD SIDE or UP facing up on the spiling template. Place the spiling template so that it is not too close to the edge of the new plank, as this will cause the saw to fall off the line. Transfer the information from the wrong side of the spiling template–UP, DOWN, FWD AFT—onto the good side of the template and planking board.

Carefully nail the spiling template to the plank with small nails hammered straight into the wood about ¼ inch in.

Make sure that the template does not move or bend. (Figure 43)

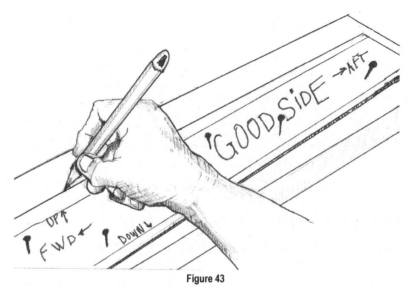

Figure 43

Spiling template is nailed to plank. Template is traced on planking board with "GOOD SIDE" facing up and "INBOARD" facing up on planking board.

MARK THE CURVE

• Trace the outline of the template onto the **inboard** side of the new board with a sharp carpenter's pencil held close to the edge of the spiling template.

• You should end up with one sharp, clear line. Check to see if the outline of the spiling template appears clearly on the planking board.

• Check any angles at the butt ends or stem or transom of the planks with your bevel gauge and extend the lines to the edge of the board so you know where to start the saw-cut.

PLANKING BEVELS

As for planking bevels, a very simple method of dealing with these is to make a miniature square that will fit against the frame and adjacent plank edge. At each frame, check the plank bevel on the adjacent plank above and below the plank being replaced. The bevel will either be:

BEVELS greater than 90°: (Figure 44 A) use a bevel gauge to transfer all these greater than 90° bevels onto a scrap piece of paper. Then find the greatest angle over 90°. This will be the bevel that allows the plank to be cut to the greatest outboard width. This will be the setting of the saw blade angle that will cut out the new plank. Now you can see why it is so important to reverse the template; if you are not keeping track of which side of the plank is which, there is a greater chance of cutting the bevel in the wrong direction. Any of the other angles greater than 90° but less than the greatest angle will be found and corrected when planing the tight spots of the plank while fitting it.

BEVELS less than 90°: (Figure 44 B) this bevel must be planed or sanded off the adjacent plank or you're never going to get the new plank in. Remember it is very important that the new plank fit tightly against the inboard edges of the adjacent planks. Do not disturb the inboard edges of the adjacent planks when planing off the bevel because you've already used these for spiling.

BEVELS very close to 90°: leave any bevels that are very close to 90° alone. (Figure 44 C)

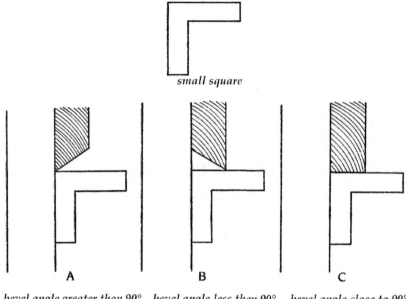

small square

A   B   C

bevel angle greater than 90°   *bevel angle less then 90°*   *bevel angle close to 90°*

Figure 44

CUTTING OUT THE PLANK

Use a circular saw with a good, sharp ripping blade and a tight guide. Set the circular saw to the corresponding greatest bevel angle that was found. That is the way the new plank must be cut. Check the angle at the saw again with the bevel gauge and make sure the angle is facing in the correct direction. *Remember that you are always working from the inboard side and the plank should be facing inboard- side-up while it is being cut.* All the bevels are measured from the inboard side. If no bevels were found greater than 90°, set the saw blade angle to 90°.

• Set the depth of the blade just a little deeper than the thickness of the plank (about ⅛-inch).

152

• Wear safety goggles; if they are scratched, dirty, or have paint splatters on them, buy a new pair.

• Make sure all lines extend all the way out to the end of the plank so you know where to start the cut.

• Start the cut just leaving the line. Make sure the saw cord doesn't stop you short in your cut and that it is clear to follow your saw all the way to the end of the cut.

• Hold the table of the circular saw with your other hand, ready to push the saw away from the line if the blade gets too close to the inside of the line. Look at the saw from the side so you can clearly watch the blade and the line. Go *slowly*. (Figure 45)

Figure 45

Cut to the outside of the pencil line. One hand guides the saw, ready to move it away or towards the pencil line if necessary. Always wear goggles.

153

• Cut one butt end of the plank that is nearest the bow or stern. You will start fitting the plank at the end that has the most curve. Cut along the line leaving the other end about 5 inches longer than the line marked.

After it is completely cut out, lay the new plank on its edge between two blocks of wood nailed to the work table. These are called cleats. Or position it between the jaws of a wood vise. Plane or sand off the saw ridges and bumps and any traces of the pencil line.

If the plank was cut to 90° because no bevels were found in the adjacent planks, make sure that the plane is held square to the plank. Do not alter the bevel that was cut into the new plank edges. You can C-clamp a batten to the plane as an edge guide. (Figures 46 and 47)

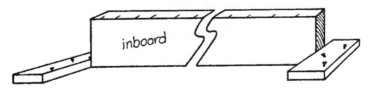

Figure 46
Wooden cleats hold the plank while it is planed.

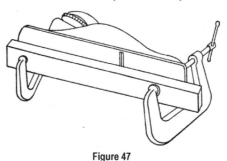

Figure 47
Clamp an edge guide to a hand plane for planning the caulking bevel.

CHECKING FOR HOLLOW

Planks at the turn of the bilge usually have to seat on frames that are curved, not flat. Lay a straight piece of doorskin along the forward side of the frame and trace the curve with a pencil.

Cut out the curve and use the convex side to simulate the curve of the frame. Use this template (or a finger-templating tool) as a guide while hollowing out the inboard side of the new plank with a grinder or a round-sole plane. Or grind the curve out of the frame.

Compare this curve with the other frames and adjust the hollow on the inboard face of the new plank accordingly.

FITTING THE PLANK

Start with the bow or stern or the end of the plank with the most hull bend. Fit the end of the plank into the plank opening. If it doesn't quite fit because there is some dirt or a glob of paint in the way, clean it out. Use a slick or chisel to take off a bump in the paint or if that won't fit in, take out the blade of the block plane and use it to fair out the lump.

If the plank is just ever so slightly too big for the opening, the edge of the plank will be marked with paint where it is tight. Use your plane to plane the plank down a little bit then try to fit it in again. Check both upper and lower edges for paint marks. Keep fitting and carefully planing until the end of the new plank fits all the way in. You may have to hang the other end of the plank with a rope to support it while fitting in one end of the plank.

If the spiling template was made correctly and not bent to fit the hole, the new plank will fit perfectly. Wedge the end of the plank in tightly against the butt block and place a screw jack or shore against it as you move along the plank fitting it in. The new plank must be seated all the way against the frames before it is fastened. Use screw jacks or shores and wedges to seat the plank tightly against the frames. Go along the plank tapping it gently to mark the tight spots and plane each one down (careful not to take too much off the plank) until it fits all the way in against the frames.

Do not hammer the tight-fitting plank into the hole. This will crush or peel back the fibers of the adjacent plank edge and stop the new plank from fitting all the way in. Be gentle and be patient. You will be impressed by how close to a "fit" the new plank is. If anything, it will be half the pencil line width from fitting perfectly into the hole.

Mark the top and bottom edges of the plank with a series of pencil marks, starting and stopping where the plank doesn't fit into the hole. (Figure 48)

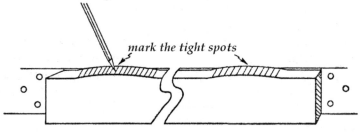

mark the tight spots

Figure 48
Fitting the new plank

Keep marking and fitting the plank. When it all fits into the opening, let the long end hang out. Make sure that the other end is all the way to the other end of the opening. Tap it with a block of wood and a mallet, if necessary, to drive it all the way tight against the adjacent butt. Wedge the long end of the plank tight against the butt end. Mark the inboard side and edges of the plank with two marks, top and bottom, where the new plank touches the butt of the adjacent plank. (Figure 49)

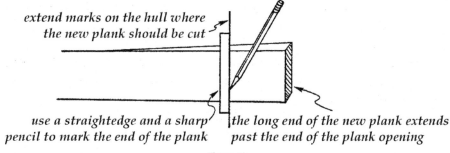

extend marks on the hull where the new plank should be cut

use a straightedge and a sharp pencil to mark the end of the plank | *the long end of the new plank extends past the end of the plank opening*

Figure 49
Mark the end of the plank

Remove the plank. Join the two marks on the inboard side of the plank and check for bevel. Cut the plank at the appropriate bevel along the line and fit it into the opening. This cut is usually 90°. Paint the end-grain of the new plank.

GAPS

If, while sighting along the edges of the new plank, you are horrified as you notice a ¼-inch gap, don't commit suicide. If the rest of the plank fits well, mark the width and length of the gap on the plank. Remove the plank from the opening. Cut out a piece of wood *from the same board* from which you cut the plank. Epoxy and C-clamp it onto the edge of the plank where the gap is. After the epoxy dries, take the C-clamp off and fair in the shim. Or make a new plank, whichever your conscience will permit.

However, if there are many areas like this that have gaps, you've been too careless planing, cutting out the plank, or spiling the template. You will have to start over again, make a new template, and cut out a new plank. Take your time. Be careful.

THE CAULKING BEVEL

Mark "OUTBOARD" on the side of the plank that will be facing outboard. Also mark TOP, BOTTOM, FWD and AFT. Examine the planks above and below where the new plank will go to determine if there is an adequate caulking bevel on those seams already. One caulking bevel per seam is usually sufficient.

If it is necessary to plane caulking bevels on the new plank, mark the depth of the caulking bevel on the edges of the new plank. The caulking bevel should extend in to ½ of the thickness of the new plank. Mark the words "CAULKING BEVEL" on the outboard half of the line. *Be careful not to bevel the wrong side of the plank.*

On the outboard side of the plank, mark a line that is ⅛-inch in from the edge (a little more for thicker planking). The caulking bevel should be at a 4° to 7° angle to the edge of the plank. The width of the caulking seam should be the same as the original caulking seams on the other hull planks. These marks will be a guide for planing in the caulking bevel. (Figure 50)

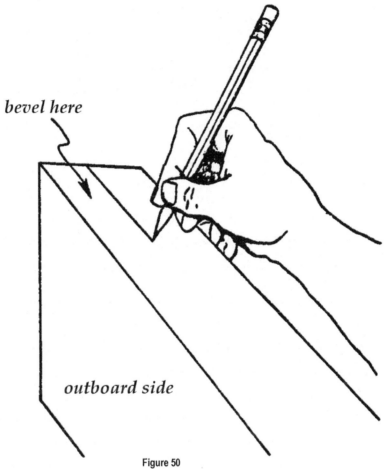

bevel here

outboard side

Figure 50
Mark the caulking bevel on the outboard half of the plank.

Set the blade of the plane.

C-clamp a piece of wood onto the bottom of the plane so the length of the exposed blade is the same as the width of the caulking bevel. This will be your caulking bevel guide. (Figure 51)

159

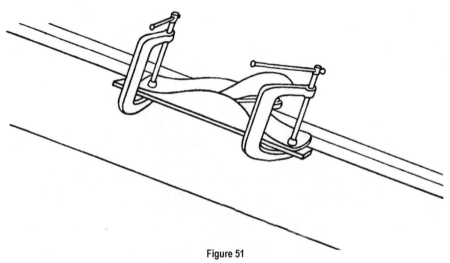

Figure 51

A piece of wood is C-clamped to the base of a block plane for planing a uniform caulking bevel.

Place the plank between the cleats nailed to the work table.

Hold the plane at the correct angle on the side of the line marked for the CAULKING BEVEL. Plane in the bevel to the lines marked. The caulking bevels at the butt ends of the plank can be formed with a belt sander. Use a fine grit sanding belt. Go slowly, be careful not to sand outside the lines marked. If the bevels at the butt ends of the planks must be hand planed, use a shallow-angled block plane and plane from the ends toward the middle of the bevel. Set the sharp blade so that it makes a very shallow cut, to avoid splitting the edges.

Paint the butt ends of the plank with red lead or other oil-base paint. This will stop them from absorbing fresh water (from the inside of the hull) that might cause them to rot.

Fasteners. If the boat is bronze screwed or copper nailed, use silicon bronze, flat head, wood screws. Use #12 screws for

1-inch planking; #14 or #16 for thicker planking. Lag bolts and washers can be used in planking 2 inch thick or thicker. A good general rule, when in doubt, is to use one size bigger diameter than that of the fasteners used in the original construction. If the boat is iron fastened, use #316 grade stainless steel flat head wood screws if possible.

If you have the money—and if you can find them—flat-head, Monel wood screws are the very best. In the long run, it always pays to use Monel and not galvanized steel or bronze.

Draw a fastener diagram to scale on a sheet of paper. Show the thickness of the frame, the thickness of the plank, and mark the depth of the countersunk hole (about ¼ of the thickness of the planking). From the drawing determine the length of the screws. Roughly they should be a little longer than twice the thickness of the plank and penetrate through ¾ of the frame. *(When fastening anything, a general rule is that the length of the fastener should equal at least twice the thickness of the thing being fastened.)* Three fasteners per plank should be used per frame for planks 3- to 6-inches wide. Four fasteners per frame can be used for planking over 6 inches wide. **Never** refasten a plank by putting a fastener into the frame only in the middle of the plank. This will cause the plank to cup. For more information on types of fasteners and refastening see the chapter on *Refastening*.

FASTENING THE PLANK STEP-BY-STEP

Start at the bow or stern end of the plank or the end that has the most hull bend. Use bedding compound or thick paint behind the plank at the butt ends, on butt blocks, on stem or stern rabbets, and at the deadwood.

Tap on the end of the plank with a hammer, using a block of wood as a pad. Make sure the plank is seated and touching the end. Don't force it if it's tight. Plane it some more if necessary.

The places where you'll be putting in the fasteners are already marked on the plank above and below. Mark these places on the new plank.

If using a #12 wood screw, you'll need a ½-inch countersunk hole. Use a spade, fly, or wood bore drill bit (they are all the same type of bit but they have three different names). Be careful when using the type of countersunk bit that goes on the tapered drill bit with Allen head set screws. These have a nasty habit of traveling up the bit as they get hot and expand. It is much better to take your time and change the drill bit between countersinking and drilling tapered holes, or you can have two drills set up: one for countersinking, one for tapered-hole drilling.

Mark the spade bit with paint or a piece of masking tape at the right depth (about ¼ of the thickness of the planking, less for softwood planking). Drill the hole just deep enough to countersink a wood plug over the head of the screw.

Drill the screw hole using a tapered drill bit for the correct screw size. Drill the holes slightly angled toward the center of the frame. If the frames are very hard, you'll have to drill in a little and pull out while the drill's still turning to clean out the drill bit, and then drill deeper till you're at the right depth. The correct depth can be marked on the drill bit with paint or masking tape.

Tap on the plank with a mallet to make sure that the plank is seated tightly against the frames. Relying on the fastener to pull it in may split the plank. This also puts too much load on the fastener and may cause it to strip out of its hole or cause the plank to cup outwards later as the fastener corrodes or stretches. (Figures 52 and 53)

Figure 52
Seat the plank tight against the frames with a block and mallet.

163

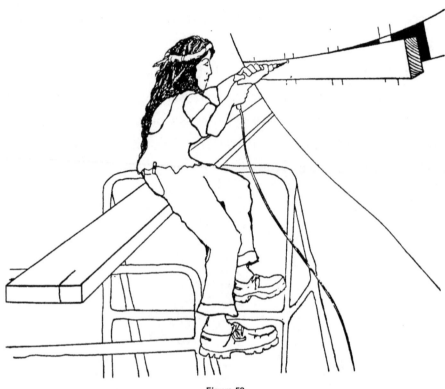

Figure 53
Where there is a lot of hull bend, start at one end seating and fastening the plank in one direction.
Use shores and wedges, if necessary, to seat the plank tightly against the frames.

Do *not* fasten the very end fastener first, especially in a stem or stern plank where it tapers off to a point. This may cause the plank to split at the end. Fasten, instead, the second-from-the-end fastener first. (Figure 54)

Dip the screw in epoxy or beeswax or other lubricant. Use a brace and screwdriver bit to tighten the screw. *Don't use an electric screwdriver.* (Nowhere in this book does it say to go fast.) You have to get the *feel* of how the screws are going in and how tightly you are setting them up. You'll get much more control and torque out of a brace and bit than from an electric screwdriver, and you won't mess up the head as much or gouge the wood if you slip. (Figure 55)

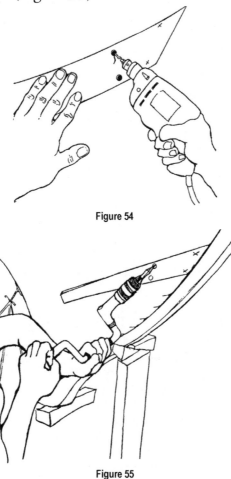

Figure 54

Figure 55

Use a brace and bit to fasten the screws for the new plank.
Start with the second fasteners from the end to avoid splitting the plank end.

Tighten up these screws.

Go along the plank tapping it in with a hammer and a

block of wood. Make sure that the plank is seated before you fasten it in. Do *not* rely on the fasteners to pull the plank in.

If the plank is a long one or if there is a lot of hull bend, you will need a screw jack and wedges to help seat it. Sometimes it is necessary to steam bend the plank around the hull curve. If you have no screw jacks, cut a 4 x 4 so that it goes from the ground up to the hull. You'll need to nail a deck cleat (block of wood) against the base of the 4 x 4 so it doesn't slip out at the bottom. Bend the plank in by hand and use the 4 x 4 with a wedge and pad to seat the plank all the way into the opening. Make sure the plank is seated before fastening it. (Figure 56)

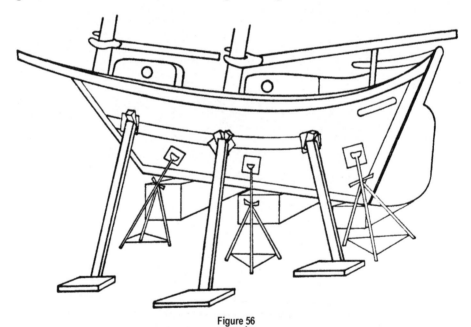

Figure 56

4 x 4 shores and wedges can be used to seat a plank.

ALL THREAD REDIROD—WHEN ALL ELSE FAILS

Redirod is all-thread or threaded stock. Redirod is used on very thick planking that is hard to bend around hull curve.

Fit in the end of the plank starting from the end that has the most hull curve (usually work from the ends of the hull towards the middle). Tap in the end; make sure it seats. Drill and fasten a frame or two back from the end.

Tap on the plank and seat it in as far as you can and fasten it in until you need the help of a redirod. Find a place between two sets of frames and wedge the new plank in as far as you can with screw jacks or 4 x 4s and wooden wedges.

Drill a hole big enough to thread the redirod through the plank and, if there is ceiling (an inner layer of planking inside the frames usually found on heavily constructed working craft), through this also, all the way to the inside of the boat. Insert the redirod. Use ⅜ inch or ½ inch on heavy planking.

Drill a hole of the same diameter in a 4 x 4 long enough to span a few frames. Stick it over the redirod that extends into the inside of the hull, add some large fender washers, and two lock nuts. Drill a hole in a plywood pad and place the pad over the outboard end of the redirod (on the outside of the hull). Add a big fender washer and a nut.

Then tighten the outside nut until the plank is pulled into the hole and seated.

Drill and fasten the plank to the frames where the plank is

seated tightly against the frames. Use the redirod where neces-sary. Use a sufficient pad on the outside of the plank so that you don't split the plank.

Remove the redirod.

Don't forget to plug the hole! Whittle out a dowel, drive and glue it into the hole, then countersink and glue a wood plug over it. Glue the dowel and wood plug in with epoxy. *Always cover a dowel with a wood plug.* A dowel has exposed end grain, a wood plug has none. (Figure 57)

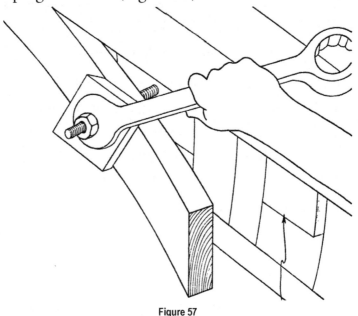

Figure 57

THE SPANISH WINDLASS

Sometimes when fitting in a topside plank or where it is impossible to use a 4 x 4 shore or screw jack, you'll have to use a little ingenuity.

Run a line (strong rope) around the whole boat: over the new plank, over the deck, under the boat up the side, over the deck, and around again. Tie off the two ends.

Place a strong stick or steel bar between the two lines and, turning the bar, twist the rope tighter and tighter. This will pull the plank in towards the opening.

After the plank is as far in as it's going to go, tie the bar off. Be careful; if it gets loose, it'll clobber you.

Then drive wooden wedges (use a plywood pad to protect the plank from splitting) between the rope and the plank to force the plank the rest of the way in, until it seats tightly on the frame. *Be careful!*

Drill and fasten the plank. Repeat where necessary. (Figure 58)

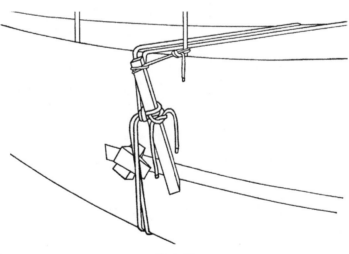

Figure 58

A Spanish windlass and wooden wedges can be used to force the end of the plank against the frames before the plank is fastened. Be sure to secure the end of the windlass bar so it doesn't smack you!

Check the plank from inboard to make sure it is seated tight against the frames before fastening.

STEAM-BENDING THE PLANK

If there is just too much bend in the plank and there is no other way to make the plank bend into place cold, the plank will need steam-bending. Put the plank into a steam box as described in Chapter 6 and steam it for at least one hour per inch of thickness. As soon as the plank comes out of the steam box, induce a bend, bring it over to the hull and wedge it into place. (Figure 13, steambox, p. 80)

Plastic Bag Steam Box – Steam Bending In Place

If the plank is too thick to bend into where it is needed and there is not enough time to get a steamed plank from the steam box to the boat before it cools, it may be smarter to steam the plank in place.

Amazon.com sells rolls of "6 mil poly tubing" - clear plastic tubing in 6 inch, 8 inch and 12 inch widths - essentially an open-ended sock made out of clear heavy plastic that fits over the plank that will become the steam-in-place steam box. Pull this plastic tubing over the plank, tape the ends closed, allow for a little accumulated water to drip out of the lowest end and poke a hole in the top of the tubing for a steam hose and tape the tubing to the steam hose.

Wedge one end of the plank in against the butt block and as many frames as it will contact, secure it with clamps or shores and wedges or temporary fasteners, leave the other end sticking out away from the hull. Then generate steam by boiling water in a tank over a propane burner or from an electric steam generator, and let the hose fill the clear plastic tube over the plank with steam.

When the plank has steamed for an hour per inch of plank thickness or until it is flexible enough to bend it into the space where it is needed, cut away the plastic bag, be careful, the bag, steam and plank is very hot, wedge and shore or fasten it into place, when it cools, it will retain its bend.

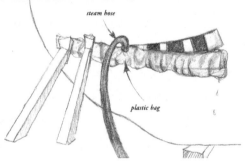

steam hose

plastic bag

Figure 59, Plastic bag steambox

PLUGGING

If you use galvanized iron screws, carriage bolts, lags, or boat nails, their heads should be painted with red lead, white lead, cold galvanizing spray, epoxy, or zinc chromate before the countersunk holes are plugged with wood plugs.

Plugs can be cut of the same wood as the planking with a plug cutter or pre-cut. If you are cutting your own, cut them from wasted planking wood. Use a drill press, then turn the board on its side and cut the plugs free on a table saw or band-saw. This method works better than using an electric hand drill to cut and a screwdriver to pry them loose. If plugs are purchased, try to get plugs of the same type of wood as that of the planking. If this is not possible, get either Honduras mahogany (red in color) or teak (brown in color) pre-cut plugs. Teak is more water resistant and does not iron sicken and absorb water. Don't use soft Philippine mahogany plugs.

Mix a batch of cabosil powder thickened epoxy glue. Turn or twist the plug into the glue until a goodly goober covers about $^{1}/_{2}$ the depth of the plug.

A little glue should be painted around the sides of the hole with a small brush or Q- tip. This will seal the end grain in the plank around the countersunk hole. When painting the glue into the countersunk plug hole with a brush or Q-tip, be careful not to put too much glue into the hole as the hydraulic pressure will not allow the plug to seat all the way in and may even push the plug out before the glue dries.

Whether the plug is of the same wood as the planking or not, it is important to match the direction of the grain of the plug with the grain of the plank. If the grain in the plug cannot be seen well enough to be sure of its direction, wet the end of the plug with glue. If you still cannot determine its direction, use another plug. Check to see that the plug is coated with glue all the way around its sides and press and hammer it lightly into the countersunk hole.

Check the direction of the grain again. If the plug needs to be turned before it is set in, use a needle-nose pliers or small vise grip to turn it. A common mistake is to confuse the saw blade marks on the plug for the grain of the wood. The saw blade marks are very often at 90° to the true grain and this won't be noticed until the plug is sanded smooth. Check also that there is a continuous glue joint all around the plug. If there is a dry spot, pull the plug out with a needle-nose pliers. If the plug is not too mutilated by then, re-glue it; otherwise, use a new plug

Tap the plug in gently with a hammer or mallet to seat it. Wipe up the excess glue from around the plug with a rag and some alcohol or thinner, but do not remove any of the glue from around the glue joint.

After the glue dries, the plugs can be faired in with the rest of the hull. This can be done with a chisel; however, great care must be taken not to break the plug off below the surface of the planking. For this reason it is safer to hand-plane the plugs or to use a slow speed soft foam pad grinder with an 80 or-100 grit sanding disc to fair in the new plank and sand the plugs down at the same time.

Puttying instead. Polyester putties do not adhere well to wet wood, and cause the wood below to rot, therefore ***Bondo and the like should never be used on a wooden boat***. If using wood plugs is impossible due to severely misshapen countersunk holes, then a putty can be made by thickening epoxy glue with colloidal silica or fine dry sawdust. If epoxy putty is used over the fastener, it is advisable to first paint around the inside of the countersunk hole with thin epoxy glue on a paint brush or Q-tip. This will improve adhesion of the putty and seal the end grain of the plank in the countersunk hole.

FAIRING IN THE PLANK

The new plank can be rough-faired with a hand or power plane and finished with a slow speed 10-inch soft foam pad grinder and 100 or 80-grit sanding discs held <u>square and flat</u> to the surface. Take down the wood plugs at the same time, holding the foam pad flat on the plank and going from the new plank towards the old planks, until the new plank is level with the rest of the planking. It is more important that you do not grind too much wood away than that the hull is perfectly fair. Excessive fairing of the hull with a grinder will remove too much wood from the planking. The plugs are made thinner; the glue around them is heated and weakened by the heat from grinding; the caulking seams are widened; there is less seam compound in them; and the fasteners are brought closer to the surface as the planks are sanded thinner to make them fair.

Never use hard pad discs in electric grinders to fair a wooden boat! These will make lumpy ridges and grooves that are too deep to fair in.

Wear protective clothing while grinding—especially when grinding bottom paint. Wear a dust mask, goggles and a barrier cream on your skin. A cool shower taken afterwards will wash the toxic chemicals from your skin without opening your pores as a hot shower would.

REMOVING WOOD PLUGS

When removing plugs, a small slot screwdriver can be driven into the center of the plug and, with a twisting motion, turned out from the countersunk hole with no damage to the head of the fastener. Never drive or pry from the edge of the plug toward the middle as this will deform the edge of the hole and make subsequent setting of plugs more difficult. If the hole needs to be re-drilled for a larger plug, it may be necessary to glue in a wood plug, fair it and re-drill through the plug to center the drill bit.

13

CAULKING

SWELLING UP

If the boat is excessively dried out so that there are checks in the surface of the planks and in the deadwood and daylight can be seen through the plank seams from the inside, it is a good idea to set up a soaker. This can be made by running saltwater through a soaker-type garden hose or lawn sprinkler set up under the boat at night for a week or two before launching.

Soaker hoses have tiny holes in them and are plugged at one end. They may be hung from scaffolding and positioned so that they spray directly onto the hull. If the boat is near salt water, rig up a pump and run a hose to the boat. Lightly salted wet burlap bags can be placed in the bilge to keep them damp; however, do not fill the bilge with water! Burlap bags can also be sewn together and placed on the outside of the hull in order to keep water from the sprinkler or soaker hose close to the wood. Sheets of plastic can be draped around the boat and a humidifier, steam generator, or steam cleaner can be set up under the boat. Whichever method is used, an attempt to swell up the hull should be made before caulking and seam compounds are applied to the seams.

Structural damage can result by adding additional caulking to a very dry boat or by caulking the boat when it is too dry, especially if the planking is hardwood. Softwood like cedar and cypress will compress, but hardwood planking if over-caulked or caulked too tightly when the boat is dry can crack frames, pull fasteners, and lift covering boards when the boat swells after launching. The seams should be blown out with an air hose or vacuumed to remove paint flakes or dirt that might prevent the planks from swelling up.

Broken or cracked stopwaters should be driven out and re-placed. Stopwaters are usually found under the planks where deadwood or stem or stern timber joints penetrate into the hull. Stopwaters need to be replaced or installed if they are deterio-rated or are absent before the new plank is fitted and fastened. The hole may need to be re-drilled and a new stopwater made out of a soft, multi-sided, hand-whittled, cedar dowel driven tight and dry into the stopwater hole, and the overhanging ends trimmed off flush with the hull. The stopwater should be ap-proximately the same diameter as the thickness of the planking.

If a plank is split or cracked from excessive dry out, as an alternative to replacing it, the crack can be filled with soft seam compound or cabosil-thickened antifouling paint. It will also help to drill and plug the two ends of the crack so that the crack does not continue to spread. It is ultimately best to replace any cracked plank if it is cracked all the way through.

Small cracks in the surface of the below-the-waterline planks should be filled with anti-fouling paint thickened with Cabosil (colloidal silica) and pressed into the crack with a putty knife or glue spreader. Wood plugs that are loose, cracked, or have dry glue joints should be removed and replaced.

CAULKING THE SEAM

It is important to use clean, dry cotton. A caulking bag or bucket will keep the cotton clean and dry.

Use a #0, #00, or #01 caulking iron depending on the width of the caulking seam. If you don't have a caulking mallet, use an ordinary leather, wood, plastic, heavy hammer, 3-pound sledge, or lead mallet—whichever works for you. I prefer the short-handled sledge or a caulking mallet.

Hammer a tapered wedge-shaped "Making iron" (also called a "dumb iron") in by itself to a depth of about ½ the depth of the seam for the entire length of the seam. This depth may be marked on the iron with a pencil. Go all along the seam and butts from one end to the other with the tapered making iron and mallet before caulking with cotton. This is called "making the seam." By driving the iron in by itself all along the seam at a constant depth, the caulking seam is made uniform and any tight spots are made wide enough to accept the cotton. Mark the loose seams with a chalk line to tell you where to use more cotton.

Lift and tuck—this is how to caulk. Leave a tapered 5 inch tail and start by jamming the cotton into the seam with the corner of your caulking iron. Tap it in about ½ the thickness of the plank with the caulking iron and mallet (Figure 60). It may help to draw or scratch a mark in the caulking iron with an awl, the depth of the caulking seam. This will be your depth gauge.

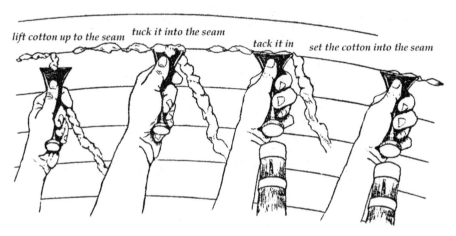

Figure 60
Follow the correct caulking bevel angle. Be sensitive. Look at and feel what you are doing, make your loops the right size to lay into the seam smoothly and at the right depth.

After the cotton is tacked in a little way from its end, reach down about an inch, lift the cotton with the caulking iron up into the seam, leaving a little tuck or loop sticking out and set the cotton again with the corner of the iron. If the seam is marked wide, leave a bigger loop. Go on lifting and tucking leaving loops in between for 5 or 6 feet along the seam, each tuck about ½ the length of the loop. Then go back to the beginning or where the loops start and, holding the caulking iron flat in the seam, drive the line of cotton (loops and all) to the depth marked on the caulking iron. Work only in one direction. Tack the cotton in loops then set the loops in to the proper depth. Set the cotton in to a smooth, even depth all along the seam.

If the cotton breaks or if you come to the end of a strand, taper both ends, twist them together, and continue. (Figure 61)

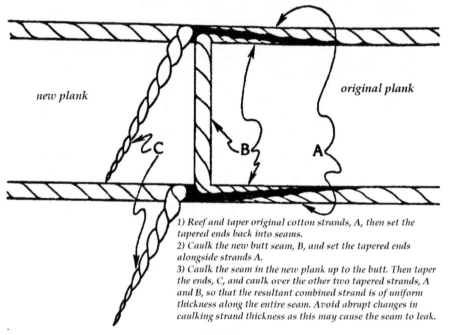

new plank

original plank

C   B   A

1) *Reef and taper original cotton strands, A, then set the tapered ends back into seams.*
2) *Caulk the new butt seam, B, and set the tapered ends alongside strands A.*
3) *Caulk the seam in the new plank up to the butt. Then taper the ends, C, and caulk over the other two tapered strands, A and B, so that the resultant combined strand is of uniform thickness along the entire seam. Avoid abrupt changes in caulking strand thickness as this may cause the seam to leak.*

Figure 61

Some people like to roll the cotton. Some use it straight. Both ways work.

When you come to a butt block, caulk the vertical seam, leave the tapered ends of cotton sticking out. Reef out the seam about 6 inches past the butt of the old adjacent plank, taper and leave out that end, then thin out the cotton strand and caulk over the tapered strands. Taper the end of the caulking so that it feathers into the remaining caulking. You should end up with a uniform evenly-caulked seam.

If the whole boat needs to be caulked, an attempt should be made to swell up the planking by setting up a soaker system before caulking.

After the moisture content of the wood has risen to an adequate level, caulk one plank on one side and the corresponding plank on the other side, starting at the garboard and gradually caulking up to the sheer plank on both sides alternately.

If the vessel was originally constructed without caulking, it is still necessary to make caulking bevels and drive cotton into the seams of any replacement planking. Taper both ends so a sudden change in cotton thickness does not occur. Never remove original cotton unless you are refastening or the cotton is rotten.

• *Original caulking should last the life of the boat. If someone tells you they have to caulk with cotton every haul-out, there is something else going on besides caulking; good chance the frames are rotten, or the fasteners are wasted, or both.*

When refastening and trying to wedge a sprung plank back tightly against the frames, it will be necessary to remove the cotton and replace it with new cotton after the plank is pulled back into position.

Check all the seams with a knife when you first haul to make sure none of the original caulking is missing or was forgotten. It is common to find butt block and seam cotton forgotten and missing. The knife should only go about half-way the thickness of the plank. Mark any places in the seams where the knife goes all the way through the thickness of the plank, pull out the tails of the adjoining cotton, taper and twist new cotton and caulk those forgotten areas.

Strands of cotton may be added where the seam widens. More strands of cotton may be added or twisted in to make a thicker strand. Any changes in thickness must occur gradually and smoothly. If the seams widen, closer spacing of the loops and additional strands with tapered ends are necessary. If the seam narrows, the strand can be made thinner and the loops made shorter between tucks. When caulking planks at the bow, or sternpost or dead-wood, leave the ends sticking out and tapered, and run a row of cotton down the stem seam or stern seam over the tapered ends. When caulking the garboard, use a "bent iron" to get the correct angle of the caulking seam.

Paying the seam. After the caulking is done and inspected, the caulking cotton must be painted with red lead, bottom paint or any good, thick enamel paint using a small paint brush. At least two good coats of paint should be put on over the cotton so that the cotton is sealed. This glues the cotton into the seam and keeps it dry and in place. It is very important to get enough paint on the cotton before the sun sets and the cotton collects moisture. If the cotton gets wet it will always wick moisture.

CAULKING REPAIRS TO LEAKY SEAMS

Before attempting to caulk a boat that leaks at the seams, first determine if the planks are well fastened. It is not correct to assume that driving more cotton into the seams of a hull that needs refastening will hold it all together. When the boat is hauled, the planking is being compressed by the weight of the boat. If the fasteners are tired or not holding the planks securely when the vessel is in the water (and not compressed by sitting on its keel out of the water), the seams may still leak no matter how much cotton you can pound in especially if the boat is working or flexing in a sea.

• *Caulking is not always the solution for leaking seams.*

• Tap on the plank with a mallet and hold the plank with your other hand at the same time to feel if the plank is loose, especially at the butts. Press against the plank with the butt end of a sledge or hammer and watch to see if it moves.

• Check the frames to see if they are strong and whether the frame wood is hard enough to hold fasteners securely.

• Inspect some of the fasteners in the area before attempting to caulk a leaky seam.

• *Driving in more cotton may just be driving the planks farther apart.*

Strong fasteners and good hard frame wood will hold your boat together when you need it held together most. Don't depend on cotton and store-bought compounds to do the work of good sound wood and strong fasteners.

When polysulfides and polyurethanes first appeared in the 1960s and 1970s, it was thought that these new compounds were miracle formulas for curing leaky seams. It was even thought that the use of cotton was no longer necessary. Cotton was reefed from the seams and these compounds squirted in with caulking guns. Although their use above the waterline on a wooden boat is sometimes acceptable, these compounds WILL cause problems when used in below-the-waterline seams.

Cotton is necessary in a carvel-planked boat that was originally constructed using cotton caulking.

As long as the caulking seams are good, the planks fit tightly on the inboard side, and the frames and fasteners are strong and holding well, cotton will tighten up the entire structure. This is something that polysulfides and polyurethanes can never do. These rubbery compounds can hide voids and trap air bubbles that will give way under pressure when the boat is in the water and flexing, causing the seams to leak. Even if applied to dry wood, there is no way of knowing what they will do when the wood is wet and the boat is flexing. If there is a leak, it will be a serious one if these compounds alone are depended upon to keep the seams glued together. I've seen wooden boats hauled out and long strings of 5200 fall out of the seams.

Do NOT use 5200 or any polyurethane products on or below the waterline seams on a wooden boat.

REPAIRING DAMAGED CAULKING SEAMS —INSTALLING "GUMP WEDGES"

If the caulking seams are too wide to hold caulking from going through to the inside of the hull, the seams will need to be repaired or the plank replaced. If the seams are too far gone to be caulked with cotton, they may be routed out with a router. A router guide nailed to the hull will keep the router on a straight course. Epoxy a length of the same wood as the original planking to the routed edge. On the other edge is a caulking bevel which is caulked with cotton like the other seams. After the epoxy dries, the spline is planed and sanded fair to the hull. The splines are best if glued only on one edge and caulked on the other. One spline glued on both sides into a seam on an otherwise caulked hull will cause problems (Figure. 62). Ultimately, the best and most permanent solution for fixing bad caulking seams is to replace the entire plank.

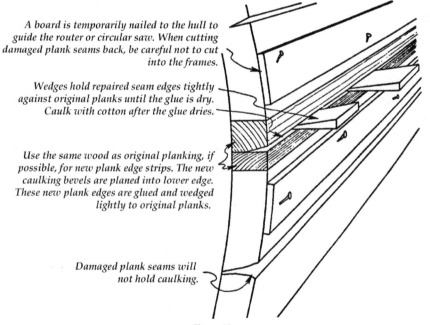

A board is temporarily nailed to the hull to guide the router or circular saw. When cutting damaged plank seams back, be careful not to cut into the frames.

Wedges hold repaired seam edges tightly against original planks until the glue is dry. Caulk with cotton after the glue dries.

Use the same wood as original planking, if possible, for new plank edge strips. The new caulking bevels are planed into lower edge. These new plank edges are glued and wedged lightly to original planks.

Damaged plank seams will not hold caulking.

Figure 62
Repairing damaged plank seams; Gump Wedges

UNDERWATER SEAM COMPOUNDS

You've fitted, plugged, raised the moisture content of the wood, caulked, painted, and faired. Now, you're wondering what type of seam compound to use. I personally mistrust using any magic-in-a-can seam compound found on the shelves of a marine store.

I know that some of you have your own opinions about what to do and what not to do, what to use and what not to use on a wooden boat. I also know that some of your opinions might differ from the methods described herein. All that I can ask is that your opinions come as a result of carefully observing those methods which have passed the test of sea and time.

IF THE BOAT HAS NOT DRIED OUT— HARD SEAM COMPOUNDS

An attempt should be made to swell up the hull before caulking and hard compounds are put into the seams, especially if the boat has been out of the water for a period of time. If the boat was planked with narrow planks, 4 inches wide or less, any new planks that were put in were selected carefully for stable wood and quarter-sawn grain, and the boat has not dried out or lost a great amount of its moisture content, then use hard or semi-hard seam compounds. Using hard compound (Splash Zone epoxy compound) or semi-hard compound (bottom paint thickened with cement to the desired consistency) in the caulking seam does not stop the planks from swelling up since only about $\frac{1}{3}$ of the outboard widened edge has compound in it and the remaining $\frac{2}{3}$ of the plank can still swell up around the cotton.

Cement

It is usual practice to use Hydraulic Portland cement in the seams (after the cotton is well painted) of "wet" wooden vessels on the Pacific Coast. A "wet" boat is one that lives all its life in the water except for a brief yearly haul-out. Some insurance companies won't insure a commercial wooden boat unless cement or hard compound is used in the seams.

The cement is double mixed. It is mixed once with water. Then, before it hardens up, it is mixed again. This time one tablespoon of linseed oil for every quart of cement is mixed in with it. This mixture is then pressed into the seams with a putty knife and painted with bottom paint as soon as the cement starts to harden.

If the cement in the seams is left to dry in the air, it will crack. It must dry slowly. Sometimes the cementing is done just before launching so that the cement can harden or "cure" under water, where it will become hard as a rock.

One boat owner insisted that the under water planks needed to expand and contract and he put soft compound in the seams of his wooden boat. Under water planks, however, do not expand and contract, they just expand and stay expanded as long as the boat is in the water. He insisted that all his boat-building friends in Maine buy a big tub of window putty or use something even softer for the seams. The seams of his wooden boat leaked and his bilge pumps ran all the time. Beware of free advice!

For those of you who are still skeptical about using cement or hard compound in the under-water seams, this was taken from the records of Percy and Small shipyard in 1909 regarding the building of the schooner WYOMING, the largest 6-masted cargo schooner ever built: "*Then came the caulkers, working upward from the garboard seam, first driving in the cotton and finally sealing the seams with Portland cement.*"

Splash Zone Compound

Splash Zone Compound is a two-part epoxy-catalyzed lead compound that was developed for the oil companies for coating the splash zone (waterline, where the worst type of corrosion occurs) on steel oil rigs. It was especially formulated so that it can be mixed and applied under water. Splash Zone will harden underwater and, unlike epoxy glues, it is not as brittle. Splash Zone can be used for seam compound especially in locations where there is a high risk of attack by marine borers entering through the seams.

Splash Zone Compound is made by several major paint manufacturers. It is also made by International Brolite. It is an equal, two-part compound. One part is black and sticky, the other part is yellow and very sticky. A golf-ball sized amount of the two parts are mixed together in water until they turn a uniform green color and kept wet in a bucket of water, then rolled into a worm and pressed well into the seam with a putty knife and scraped off the surface. Keep Splash Zone Compound wet until it is where you want it.

When using Splash Zone Compound in the seams over painted cotton, the excess green-colored epoxy should be sanded after it hardens so that bottom paint will adhere to it. Splash Zone Compound is also very useful for emergency underwater repairs when the boat is back in the water and underway.

IF THE BOAT HAS DRIED OUT

Semi-hard Seam Compounds for Below the Waterline

Before caulking a dry boat, it should be made to regain some of its moisture content by use of a soaker system. Semi-hard seam compounds can be made by using Portland cement, but adding antifouling bottom paint. The softer the compound that is needed, the more bottom paint is added to the cement. This is used if the boat has been hauled out for a long time or is taken out of the water for the winter.

If the boat was planked with very wide planks (wider than 4 inches) or with a wood that swells a lot, you will want to use a semi-hard compound to allow the wood to swell and then reef it out and use hard compound in the seams the next time the boat comes out of the water.

Seam compounds should be pressed well into the seams with a putty knife or glue spreader, so that they completely cover the painted cotton and fill up the seam. It should not cover the outboard surface of the planks, only the seams.

Wet patch or plastic roofing cement or waterproof roofing tar can be used as a bedding for butt blocks, transducers, wormshoes, and structural backbone assemblies: wherever a flexible water-proof bedding compound is needed. It can be found in almost every hardware store, paint store, lumberyard and building supply store, and is very inexpensive. Mix antifouling bottom paint in with the roofing tar. Some vinyl antifouling paints may not be compatible with wet patch, and a test for compatibility should be made.

Commercial Types of Underwater Seam Compound

I have seen shipworm eat through Dolphinite Under-water Seam Compound, Slick Seam, through red lead painted wood, and through window putty like they use in Maine.

I have even seen shipworms eat through the fiberglass covering to get at the plywood inside a rudder.

I prefer to make my own using bottom antifouling paint thickened with cement, or Splash Zone compound.

14

THE GRAVING BLOCK

A graving block is used to replace a small area of deteriorated wood that is within a larger member of sound wood.

Use a graving block when the replacement of the entire member is either inappropriate or unnecessary. Remove the deteriorated part, and inlay a new piece of wood in its place. The theory is that *it is always better to fix wood with wood.*

Don't dare even think of using Bondo anywhere on a wooden boat.

Only planks thicker than 1¼ inches should be repaired with a graving block.

GRAVING BLOCKS IN PLANKING: STEP BY STEP

If you don't already have one, you will need a 2-inch, ½-inch, and a 1-inch chisel.

Hollow grind a chisel on a grindstone or the round end of a belt sander, dip the end in cold water to prevent over-heating the metal and finish off on wet grinding and polishing stones. Hone new chisels on a set of water stones until they are sharp enough to shave the hair off the back of your hand. If you are having trouble keeping a constant angle when sharpening the chisel, make a sharpening guide. Don't attempt a graving block if your chisels aren't razor sharp.

Circle the soft spot. It will usually be over a deteriorated iron fastener that is "bleeding" (rust marks the spot).

With an awl or ice pick, check out the spot to determine if it is soft around the fastener and how far the soft wood extends. Draw a cross over the soft spot so that the center of the cross is in the center of the soft spot. Dig out the wood plug using a ¼-inch chisel or slot screwdriver. If there is an iron nail there, remove it and install a new fastener.

Make a handy little wire brush for cleaning the rust off the head of an iron nail by cutting a 1-inch length off some plastic-coated, ¼-inch stainless steel rigging wire. Strip one end of the plastic coating back about ½ inch to expose the end of the wire stands. This is a custom wire brush that will fit into a countersunk fastener hole. Tighten the other end of the wire, still coated with plastic shielding into the chuck of an electric drill. (Figure 63)

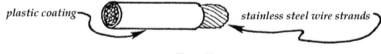

plastic coating   stainless steel wire strands

Figure 63

Make a wire brush from a short length of plastic-coated rigging wire. Strip the coating back on one end.
Use in an electric drill to clean the rust from the head of an iron fastener or if possible, remove the iron
fastener and install a new non-ferrous fastener.

Measure for and cut out a diamond-shaped piece of wood that will cover the area of soft wood and wood chewed up by the removal of the deteriorated fastener. Make this diamond shaped graving block out of the same type of wood as the planking and align its grain with the grain of the planking. (Figure 64)

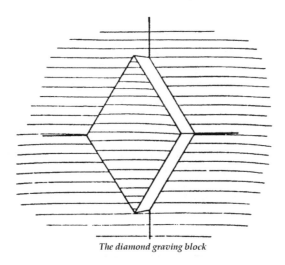

The diamond graving block

Figure 64
Grain should align and match the grain in the plank. Draw a cross through the part of the plank being repaired to center a diamond graving block

Place the wooden diamond over the soft area so that it is centered on the cross.

Hold a very sharp pencil very close to the edge of the diamond, trace its outline onto the hull.

Use a sharp knife and a square or steel straight edge to guide the knife as you cut along the line. Cut through the paint and through about ⅛ inch of wood. Be very careful not to cut past the line. (Figure 65)

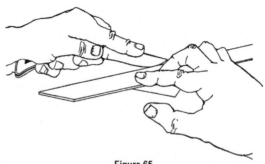

Figure 65
Cut along the outline of the diamond graving block with a knife and a steel straight edge.

Use a sharp 2-inch chisel and a heavy hammer or short-handled sledge. Place the flat side of the chisel blade into the knife cut so that the beveled side of the blade is facing the center of the diamond. Hammer the blade about ⅜ inch into the knife cut (Figure 66). (Or use a "MULTI TOOL" made by Dremel, Fein, DeWalt or Milwaukee with a wood-cutting blade instead of a chisel with good results.)

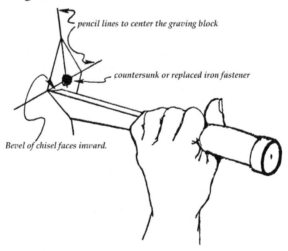

pencil lines to center the graving block

countersunk or replaced iron fastener

Bevel of chisel faces inward.

Figure 66
Inlay a diamond graving block for planking 1 ½ inches or thicker.

Use the ½-inch chisel to follow the cut made by the 2-inch chisel to a depth of ½ the thickness of the wood or the depth of the wood deterioration. Mark a line on the blade as a depth guide.

With the ½-inch chisel, or electric multi-tool chisel, going from the center outwards to the edge, carve out the bottom surface of the diamond-shaped hole. If you are very careful to keep clear of the nail and the sides, a router can be used to remove the wood from the diamond- shaped hole. Watch out for hidden fasteners. After the wood is carved out from around the nail, remove or countersunk with a spike set depending on its condition.

If you don't have one, you can make a spike set by grinding down one end of a welder's chipping hammer into a flat-ended, tapered spike. Use this to countersink nails or spikes. A bolt of the correct size or a punch held by a vise grip can also be used as a nail or spike set. (Figure 67)

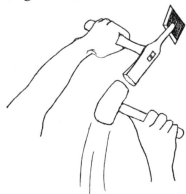

Figure 67
Countersink rust-bleeding nails deeper with a spike set or remove them, depending on their condition.

Don't bother to make the bottom of the diamond hole smooth, it will glue better if it is left rough. Make sure that the edges of the diamond graving block are smooth, straight and within the knife cut. Place the diamond graving block into the hole so that it is held in by itself. Don't hammer it in for you'll never get it out. Just place it in the hole lightly to see if it fits. There should be a half of a pencil-line-thick space around the diamond inlay. This will allow enough epoxy around the diamond graving block to insure a good glue joint.

Write something on the graving block so you'll know which way is up. Be sure that the wood is perfectly dry before attempting to glue in the diamond graving block.

Fill the countersunk nail hole with cabosil-thickened epoxy.

Spread the thick epoxy in the hole coating all five surfaces. Don't put too much epoxy in the hole as this may cause hydraulic pressure that will not allow the graving block to go all the way in. Just coat the surfaces well.

Do the same for the diamond graving block, coating all five inside surfaces with thickened epoxy.

Carefully hammer in the graving block using a wood pad to protect it until it bottoms out. Make sure the word you wrote on the outside is the right side up.

Clean up the area with thinner or vinegar, but don't remove any epoxy from the glue joint itself.

When the epoxy has hardened, soft pad or plane and sand

the graving block fair with the hull. Check it by running your bare hand over it to make sure it is smooth.

After soft pad grinding or planing the diamond graving block fair, check the glue joint for pin hole voids; if there are any, fill them with some epoxy on a plastic spreader.

Prime the graving block and paint with whatever paint you are using and it should disappear.

The reason we use a diamond-shaped graving block is that a square-shaped one will crack at the edges when the boat works. A diamond-shaped graving block will move with the plank, it is locked-in, and has more end-grain surface to glue.

15

REFASTENING

The signs that indicate that refastening is overdue are *hard spots* or breaks in the fair curve of the hull and *outward cupping* of the planks at their edges.

HARD SPOTS

Look for hard spots especially at the turn of the bilge. Also examine thoroughly from the inside to determine if there are broken or deteriorated frames in this area. If the fasteners are losing their grip on the frames, either the fasteners are deteriorated or the frames are. When examining the frames from the inside, look between the frames and the planks for cracks or soft wood. Look for gaps which indicate that the planks are pulling away from the frames. Probe the frames with an screw driver or knife to determine their hardness. Look for caulking cotton that has been driven through the seams. Look for rust streaks or discoloration on the inboard side of the planks near the seams. These signs may indicate that before you refasten, the frames must be replaced or repaired so that there is something solid to which the planks can be fastened.

If you find "chining" or angular planks at the turn of the bilge, check from inboard side to see if the upper and lower edges of the plank are touching the frame. If the plank only touches the frame at the middle of the plank, it is possible that the inboard side of the plank was not hollowed with a plane or sander to accommodate the curve of the frame. If this is the situation, then remove these planks and hollowed their inboard sides or make new planks that accommodate the curve of the frame (usually when you remove a plank it is better to make a new one than refasten the old one).

If the frames are bad and need replacing, turn to Chapter 10, *Laminated Frames*. This is the strongest method of framing when done correctly. If the frames appear to be good everywhere else, except for where they are severely cracked or rotten, then remove the bad sections of the frame, scarph in new sections, and install sister frames to restore continuity. Mark and cut the frames with a circular saw (blade set to the depth of the frame) to remove the deteriorated sections of frames.

If several frames sections of frames are deteriorated, do not cut all the frames along the same line. Instead, cut the frames in different places so that each frame has a different-sized section to replace. A simple 5:1 step scarf makes an excellent joint when replacing sections of the frame. (Figure 68)

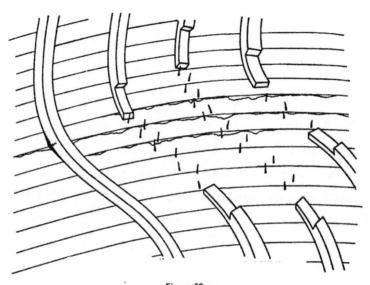

Figure 68
Remove staggered damaged frame sections in preparation for reseating sprung planks and repairing damaged frames.

After you remove the bad sections of frame and you cut step scarf notches in the remaining parts of the frame, back out the fasteners. Scrape or grind the bottom paint off the planking on the outside of the hull to expose the wood plugs over the fastener. Remove the wood plugs from the outside, hammer a screwdriver into their center, twist and dig out the plug to expose the fastener head. If the fastener is a screw, clean out the slot and try to back it out from the outside with a screwdriver that fits the head. You may need to tap the handle of the screwdriver with a hammer while turning it or use an impact driver to start the screw turning. Make sure that all the wood and glue is removed from the plug hole and that the screw is free to come out. If you are unable to back the screw out from the outside, or if the fastener is a nail, you may need to hammer it out from the

200

inside. Hold a back-up pad with a hole drilled in it against the of the plank, this may prevent the wood around it from splitting while you hammer out the fastener.

After the fasteners are backed out from where the frame sections were removed, reef the caulking out in the area of the hard spot to allow these planks to be wedged back against the sister frames. Be careful not to damage the caulking bevel and plank edges. Clean out any dirt and wood chips from the caulking seam and between the frame and plank.

Wedge back any sprung planks before refastening them to the frames. Use screw jacks or 4 x 4s cut to the right length, and nail deck cleats into the ground to stop the bottoms of the 4 x 4s from slipping out. Hammer wooden wedges with plywood pads under them against the plank to move the sprung plank to its original place. Position these wedges or screw jacks between where the frame sections and sister frames will be place so that they do not interfere with drilling and installing the new fasteners.

If wedging the planks at the hard spot doesn't help to bring them back into a fair curve, don't force them. Chances are that when the new sister frames are fastened in, this will pull the sprung planks back to where they belong. If you remove one of the sprung planks, use a C-clamp to pull the adjacent sprung planks and laminations of the laminated frame together.

Install sister frames between every frame to regain continuity. These should be as long as possible. Make laminated frames as described in the section on framing and if the curves are radical, the laminations will need to be steamed.

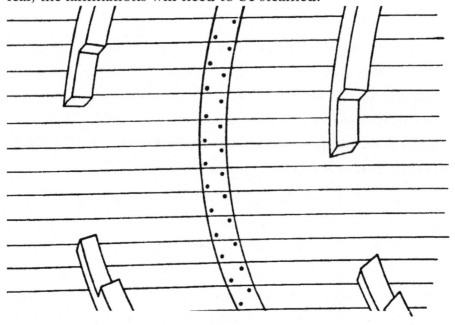

Figure 69

A sister frame is added to restore continuity. Damaged sections of original frames are removed and scarfs are made for the new frame sections. The location of the sister frames is marked and small holes are drilled from the inside.

Mark where the sisters will go from the inside by holding one of the laminations in place between two existing frames. Mark the outline with a pencil from the inside of the hull and mark where to place the fasteners. Drill fasteners slightly towards the center of the frames. Never place fasteners only in the middle of the plank as this will cause the plank's edges to cup outwards.

After you mark the location of the sister frames and fastener holes from the inside, drill holes through the planks *from the inside* with a small drill bit to mark where they will be outside. When fastening in the sister frames, start at the bottom and fasten consecutively upwards to the top. You will see the planks tightening up and the hard spot or break rounding out into a fair curve again.

After you install the sister frames, replace the frame sections where the damaged parts were removed. This can either be done by laminating the frame sections in place or sawing them out of a board of the same thickness as that of the width of the frame. The curve of the grain should match the shape of the removed frame section. After these are glued and fastened, caulk the seams carefully.

Of course the alternative and ultimately the best method to repair a hard spot or pulled planks is to remove and replace the entire frame (one at a time, or every other one in the area of the sprung planks). Then install new frames, remove the sprung planks and replace with new planks so they fit tightly against the new frames. If this method is chosen, it may help to remove one of the sprung planks first to allow the use of C-clamps from the outside to help in the fitting of the steam bent or laminated frames.

CUPPED PLANKS

It is very difficult to wedge a cupped plank back into shape. Sometimes this condition is symptomatic of deteriorating fasteners or wrongly placed planking grain and doesn't necessarily indicate deteriorated frames. If the planks are not fastened with their grain crowning outboard, the planks will cup and refastening will not remedy this situation. If your wooden boat is 20 years or older, pull and test some random fasteners if it has never been refastened. This might be the time for refastening. Examine the planking for any subtle signs that the planks are cupping outward and remove some sample fasteners from different locations for inspection. If caught early, this condition can be stopped. If allowed to continue, it will become irreversible. Refastening by only adding a fastener in the middle of the plank will make this condition worse.

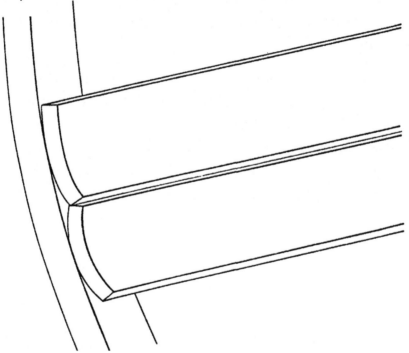

Figure 70
Cupped planks

Cupping occurs especially where the planks are wider than four inches. Narrow planks are much less prone to cupping and are much more stable. The frames should be inspected to determine whether they are in good enough condition to hold the new fasteners securely. Again, the caulking and plugs must be carefully removed. If there is a gap, clean between the frame and the plank; use a sawzall blade or hacksaw blade to remove trapped dirt. Sometimes you can tighten up the original fasteners. If they are screws, try to tighten them. If they are nails, try to set them with a hammer and spike set with someone backing them up from the inside with a sledge hammer pressed against the frame. If this doesn't help, back out the screws. Re-drill the countersunk hole if it is ragged and, using a tapered drill bit, re-drill the original hole for the next size bigger diameter screw. Use a brace and bit to tighten up the new screws.

If you decide that you want to remove the iron nail, you will need to chisel the wood around the nail head out so that you can use a pry bar, vise grip, claw hammer, or cat's paw to remove the nail. This usually makes a mess of the plank and should not be attempted unless the nails are very deteriorated. Inlay diamond graving blocks over the nail heads if the wood gets chewed up too badly by removing the nail. See Chapter 14 on *Graving Blocks.*

Wooden boats are designed and constructed so that they can be repaired. Deterioration and corrosion are always ongoing processes; through common sense and good maintenance we can keep up with them, but ultimate replacement of deteriorated parts of a wooden boat is inevitable.

Most wooden boats were designed to have one more chance at refastening before the frames are used up. If you remove some of the fasteners and determine that they are deteriorated, it is wise to remove and replace them with new fasteners. If their removal is impossible, you may elect to refasten by adding new fasteners and leaving the old ones in place (Figure 71). But you are just buying some time as it is inevitable that replacement of frames and planks will be necessary in the future. If the boat is lightly framed, the addition of new fasteners may weaken the frames to the extent that they may break. If the deteriorated fasteners are allowed to remain they will continue to deteriorate and eventually the adjacent planks and frames will need replacement. This should be considered before attempting to add new fasteners without removing the old ones.

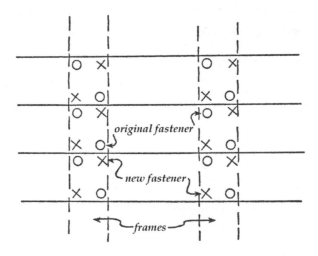

Figure 71

Whether the old fasteners are removed and replaced or additional fasteners added and the original ones allowed to remain, if the planks have started to cup, the planks will need to be replaced or refastened to stop this condition from progressing. If this condition is complicated by deteriorated wood around the fasteners, it is best to replace the cupped planking. If additional fasteners are to be added and the old ones allowed to remain, remove the paint to determine the location of the old and the placement of the new fasteners. Usually, even after refastening, the planks will still be cupped a little. It is very difficult to reverse this process. If the planks are of sufficient thickness, and the new and old plugs over the fasteners countersunk deep enough, and the planks are well seated against the frames then, the planks can be faired out with a hand plane, soft pad grinder, or fairing board and coarse sand paper. However, if the planking is less than 1¼-inch thick, fairing them out will take too much of their strength away and place the fasteners too close to the surface. Always check if the reason the planks are cupped is because their inboard sides were not hollowed for curved frames at the turn of the bilge.

Caulk the seams and install new wood plugs after the refastening has been completed. When refastening, all butt blocks must be inspected for leaking (rust streaks or water discoloration), deteriorated fasteners, cracks or rot, the absence of beveled top edges, and the absence of bedding compound. If any of these conditions are discovered, the butt block will need to be replaced. If only deteriorated fasteners are found in the butt blocks, remove the wood plug from the outside and remove the screws or carriage bolts one at a time and replace them with new carriage bolts or flat-head machine screws, washers, and nuts. Be sure to countersink the head of the bolt deep enough to be able to glue a good wood plug over it. It always good practice if replacing a plank to replace the butt blocks.

WHEN TO REFASTEN

Refastening should be attempted only if the planking and frames are still in good condition but the fasteners have deteriorated or are losing their grip.

TYPES OF FASTENERS FOR REFASTENING

Iron-Fastened Boats

If the boat was originally iron fastened, the choices of metals for refastening are: stainless steel (type #316) screws, Monel screws, Monel ring shanks, or galvanized iron boat nails.

Stainless steel screws. Stainless steel, sheet metal screws should not be used for fastening or refastening planks to frames. Flat-head wood screws should be used because, since their shanks are smooth, they are able to turn freely where they penetrate through the plank, allowing the head to pull the plank tightly against the frame. Because the threads extend all the way to the head of a sheet metal screw, the screw will tighten into the plank before it has a chance to pull the plank that extra bit tighter against the frame. This may cause a space between the frame and plank. Water may follow the threads to the space between the frame and plank and cause the screw to corrode.

Stainless steel, flat-head, type 316, wood screws are used to replace iron or galvanized steel fasteners because they are much more resistant to corrosion than steel screws and good galvanized iron screws are virtually impossible to find. Stainless steel number 316 screws are very strong and are compatible with existing ferrous fasteners and won't react adversely. However, stainless steel, when not in the presence of oxygen, may corrode by pitting caused by crevice corrosion. If stainless steel screws are used to refasten an originally iron-fastened boat, it is worth the extra research to locate a source for type #316 stainless steel, flat-head wood screws. This type is better suited for use under water. They are sometimes called 18-10-3, which represents 18-percent chromium 10-percent nickel, 3-percent molybdenum, (and of course 69-percent steel).

Monel flat-head wood screws. These are the very best choice for fastening or refastening any wooden boat. Monel is very corrosion resistant. It is made from a high percent of nickel and a lower percent of copper and is stronger and harder than bronze. Monel screws are, however, very expensive. But when considering their longevity, their cost can be justified.

Galvanized iron boat nails or square nails. It can be argued that if the boat is originally built with galvanized iron nails, it should be repaired with galvanized iron nails. Although there are far better metals for fastening wooden boats that don't cause so much wood damage, galvanized iron nails can be used for refastening an iron-fastened wooden boat. Two disadvantages of their use are: the galvanizing is often worn or broken off the head of the nail while it is being driven or set, and iron sickness and corrosion will occur and eventually deteriorate the adjacent wood. The impact from hammering and setting of the nail in an old wooden boat may jar or loosen the adjacent planks and weaken the integrity of the rest of the boat.

Galvanized iron boat nails have excellent holding power and if good iron is used they may outlast bronze fasteners. They certainly bond tighter to oak frames than do bronze screws. However, iron as it corrodes may deteriorate the adjacent wood by a chemical reaction to such an extent that replacement of frame and plank may ultimately be inevitable. The use of ferrous fasteners in mahogany planking should be avoided as this wood is particularly sensitive to the chemical reaction and deteriorates quite rapidly once corrosion begins. If the wood is black or discolored around a ferrous fastener, this does not necessarily indicate that the wood is deteriorated. If the wood around a ferrous fastener is discolored but still hard, leave it alone.

If galvanized iron boat nails must be used, they may sometimes be purchased quite inexpensively from an old boatyard that built wooden boats in the past. These nails should be hot-dipped in zinc at a galvanizing shop, never zinc electroplated. It is also advisable to dip galvanized iron boat nails in white lead, red lead, or epoxy before driving them and drive them in while their coating is still wet (red and white lead may sometimes be purchased at old boatyards or shipyards.)

Steel nails should *NOT* be used, and it is wise to test nails before purchasing them to determine if they are in fact iron or steel. The test for iron is a spark test. The metal is ground on a grind wheel and the color of the sparks observed. If the sparks are yellow-orange or red-orange, the metal is probably steel. If the sparks are white or light whitish-yellow, this indicates that the metal is probably iron.

• *Never use common galvanized steel house nails anywhere on a wooden boat.*

The shaft of a true galvanized boat nail is rectangular in section. There is a big rounded bulge on two sides of the rectangular shank below the head and the shank then tapers to a blunt or a rectangular chisel point. Blunt points hold best, but chisel points are used for clench nails. There are four distinct sharp edges on the shaft of the fastener and the head may be square or rectangular in shape. The rectangular blunt or chisel point should be driven vertical (square) to the grain of the plank wood so as not to split the wood along the grain. This will align the bulge of the shaft so that it is horizontal (parallel) to the direction of the grain of the plank.

Iron boat nails must be countersunk and drilled for their shank, using the diameter of the nail a little above the blunt point end as a reference. It is useful to drill the hole for the iron nail with a tapered drill bit for the nearest corresponding screw size, disregarding the bulge in the nail. The hole should be angled toward the center of the frame so that it enters the frame at a diagonal angle and is less likely to split the grain.

When driving the galvanized iron boat nail, the frame to which it is being fastened must be backed up from the inside by a helper, pressing against the frame with a heavy sledge hammer. When it is driven in so that its head is flush with the rest of the planking the iron boat nail should be countersunk to about ¼ of the depth of the planking with a spike set. Care must be taken not to break off the galvanizing at the head of the nail.

Bronze-Fastened Boats

• *Never use brass screws below the salt water line on a wooden boat.*

Brass is soft and will corrode more quickly than any other metal. Use silicon bronze flat-head wood screws for fastening or refastening a bronze- fastened wooden boat. Silicon bronze is made up of 96-percent copper and 4-percent silicon. When removing bronze or brass screws, if the head is mutilated, breaks off, or if the screw is stripped and won't come out, drill the recommended sized hole into the remaining part of the fastener and hammer an "easy out" or screw extractor into the hole. Then, using a vise grip, turn and pull out the screw. Remove only the screws from one or two frames at a time and replace these before removing any more. Remove the caulking and wedge the plank in tight against the frame. Use a larger diameter screw in the same hole. Before installing the new screw, check to see that there is no dirt trapped between the frame and the plank that will interfere with the plank seating tightly against the frame. A sawzall blade and a vacuum cleaner will help clean out this gap if there is one. Use a small sledge hammer and a wooden pad, or a 4 x 4 shore, pad and wedges to make sure that the plank is seated firmly against the frames before attempting to refasten a plank that has pulled away from its frame.

Copper Rivets

First inspect the rivet from the inside for corrosion or leaking. Rivets are easily removed for inspection by first removing the wood plug over the head from the outside. Then from the inside, the bulge that was formed over the washer is drilled or ground down so that the rivet may be backed out from the inside, driving it outward with a small punch and a hammer. Rivets should be inspected for brittleness and corrosion. Hold the rivet between two vise grips or in a vise and try to bend it. If it crumbles or breaks off and is pink or chalky inside, it will need to be replaced. If replacing is necessary, use a larger diameter rivet by drilling a larger diameter hole than the original.

Rivets are less expensive than screws, and because of their greater strength, a smaller diameter rivet can be used than that of a screw. Because a smaller hole can be drilled, there is less possibility of the frame splitting while the rivet is fastened than when fastening a larger screw or nail. Rivets, though, are harder to replace than screws when access is not possible from the inside due to ceilings, interior joinery, or permanent installations and machinery. Screws can be installed from the outside without disturbing inside permanent installations.

If a plank is being fastened with rivets, it may be necessary to insert a temporary through-bolt and washers to help pull the plank in tightly against the frame, fasten the other rivet in the same frame, and then replace the through-bolt with a rivet.

Drill hole for the rivet through the new plank from the inside through the original hole in the frame if the original frame is not replaced; then countersink the hole from the outside for the plug. If there is hardwood planking, the hole in the plank should be the same size as the stem of the rivet; if softwood planking, the hole in the plank for the rivet can be drilled a little smaller and a washer can be placed under the head of the rivet to give it more holding power. Drive the rivet into the hole and countersunk with a nail set or punch from the outside. Then place the washer or burr over the inboard end of the rivet from inside and, use a tool called a "hollow rove punch," to set the washer tightly against the frame. The hollow rove punch can be made by threading a nut of a larger inside diameter than that of the rivet over the end of the bolt.

When the nut is placed over the washer, the end of the rivet should not touch the end of the bolt (inside the nut). By hitting the head end of the bolt with a hammer, while the head of the rivet is backed-up from the outside, the washer is seated on the frame. Next the inboard end of the rivet is cut off about one and a half times the diameter of the rivet away from the washer, and while it is still being backed up from the outside by a helper with a punch or nail set and a hammer held on the head of the rivet, the cut-off end is rounded over the washer by lightly tapping on the end of the rivet with a ballpeen hammer. It will help to paint the inboard end of the rivet to protect it from corrosion.

Ring-shank Nails

Another type of nail commonly used in wooden boats is the ring-shank nail. These are available in bronze, stainless steel, and Monel. Monel is the most expensive and the longest lasting. Ring-shank nails have a round flat head and a shank that is smooth and notched on two sides below the head. Below the shank, are circular rings to the bottom. The tip is usually four-sided and comes to a point. All silver-colored ring shanks should be tested with a magnet before use to determine if they are simply common steel ring shanks. Steel ring-shanks should not be used.

Ring shanks should be countersunk with a wood bore drill bit and then drilled with a high-speed metal drill bit a little smaller than the shaft diameter. The frames must be backed up while these nails are being hammered in.

Bolts for Butt Blocks

When refastening or surveying the fasteners, all bolts that hold the butt blocks should be inspected for corrosion and if there is any doubt as to their condition, they should be removed, examined, and replaced if necessary. If a butt seam is wet, it would be wise to inspect the butt block fasteners before reefing and caulking. Check the threads on machine bolts and carriage bolts before buying them to be sure that they do not have expanded threads instead of cut threads (Figure 72). Expanded threads are larger in diameter than the diameter of the smooth part of the shank below the head. They may leak because the hole in the plank is enlarged by the threaded part of the bolt and does not fit tightly around the shank of the bolt. For this reason, expanded thread bolts should be avoided. Also avoid bolts that are threaded all the way up to the head. These, like sheet metal screws, may tighten into the plank before they pull the plank and butt block tightly together.

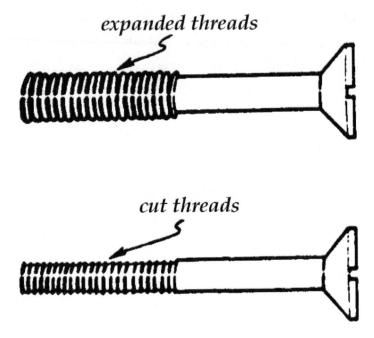

Figure 72

Expanded threads should not be used. Bolt holes may leak because the hole needed for the threads is larger than the shank.

Always use a flat washer of sufficient size behind the nut when fastening through wood. Use a grommet or washer made of caulking cotton under the head of a carriage bolt to prevent it from leaking. Screws and bolts can be coated with wet paint or grease to help lubricate them before they are driven in.

Do NOT use galvanized carriage bolts to fasten butt blocks or for refastening plank to frames.

• *Never use graphite or graphite grease on metal used under water. Graphite is the most noble of any metal and will cause accelerated corrosion of adjacent metals.*

Trunnels

Trunnels (aka: treenails) are round or tapered wooden pegs with square outboard ends with or without slots for wedges, driven into similar-shaped holes drilled in plank and frame. They should only be used on heavy sawn frames, and metal fasteners for lighter steam-bent frames. The rule of thumb, a hundred-foot boat will need 1 inch diameter trunnels, a fifty-foot boat will need ½ inch trunnels, etc. The trunnel should extend through the plank and ½ way into the depth of the frame. The plank should be tight against the frame, don't expect the trunnel to pull the plank in. Black locust is best wood for trunnels as it is rot resistant, strong and does not expand so it will not split the plank. I would avoid oak for trunnels as it is a favorite food for shipworm and I have seen trunnels eaten out by marine boring worms because they are end-grain and easy for worms to enter.

16

MAKING TEMPLATES FOR FLOOR TIMBERS

Essentially, the process for making the floor timber template is the same process as for making any other template (for shutter planks, bulkheads, king planks, covering boards, etc.) wherever changing or rolling bevels occur.

To make this whole thing a little easier, the two sides of the floor timber and floor timber template will be called:

• *inboard side*—the side facing the frame.

• *outboard side*—the side facing away from the frame.

Mark the new floor timber and cut it out with the *inboard side* facing up, that is, cut out from the *inboard side* toward the *outboard side,* and measure all bevels from the *inboard side.*

For the template, use a piece of rigid ¼-inch plywood or ⅛-inch doorskin. Use a tape measure, find the rough dimensions and cut the template out so that it will fit against the frames spanning almost all the way from side to side, with about ½-

inch space between the template and the hull planking. Secure the template to the frames with small nails.

SPILING METHODS

The Block Method

In this method, cut a small block of wood so that when placed against the hull planking it will more than span the gap between the template and the planking. Hold the block flat against the template—one edge touching the template, the other edge touching the hull—and use a sharp pencil to mark the template along the edge of the block where it touches the template.

Mark the SET on the block so that you are certain which way it was held when marking the template. It must be held the same way when transferring the marks onto the new floor timber. Write SET on the template so you can double-check it before transferring the marks onto the new floor timber. (Figures 73-74-75).

The Divider Method

Adjust a pair of locking or rigid dividers so that the points more than span the distance between the hull and the template. The point of the dividers will make a mark at a set distance all the way around the template, recording the distance between the mark on the template and the hull planking. Pencil dividers maybe used, but extra care must be taken that these do not change setting and that the pencil does not move during the

219

inboard side
outboard side

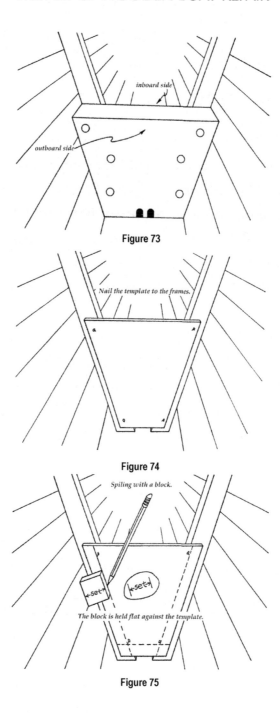

Figure 73

Nail the template to the frames.

Figure 74

Spiling with a block.
set
set
The block is held flat against the template.

Figure 75

spiling process. Mark the SET of the dividers on the template and check this occasionally to be sure that the dividers have not changed setting. Hold the dividers square to the edge of the template and mark arrows on the template to show the direction from which the marks were taken. Circle the marks. (Figure 76)

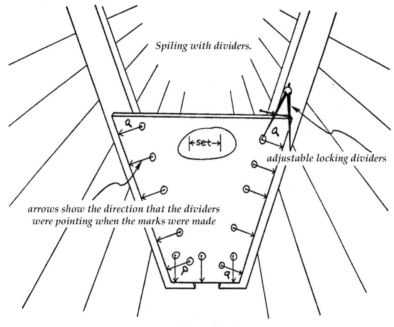

Spiling with dividers.

adjustable locking dividers

arrows show the direction that the dividers were pointing when the marks were made

Figure 76

The Stick Trick

The Stick Trick pre-dates the Stanley tape measure and is just as accurate. Although it is used for making large, complex-shaped templates like bulkhead templates, it is worth mentioning as an alternative method for making floor timber or any other templates.

In this method cut a "Stick" out of a thin piece of wood:

⅛-inch doorskln will work well. It is shaped as shown in Figure 77.

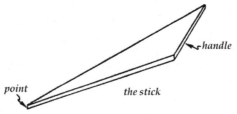

Figure 77

Trace the handle end onto the template. The shape will represent the one and only way that the stick could lay when its point recorded a significant spot. Move the stick clockwise or counterclockwise around the template and mark the angle of the handle on the template when the point of the stick touches the hull planking. (Figure 78-79)

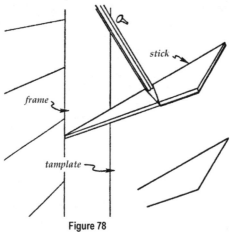

Figure 78

Form-Fitting Template

This is my favorite method and the most accurate. In this method, a template is made that is the exact shape of the new floor timber. Cut the template out of ⅛ inch doorskin or thin plywood, so that it roughly fits into the space where the new floor timber will live with a ½ inch gap all around it. Nail it to the frames so that it will not move. Then fill the valleys or spaces between the template and the hull planking with strips of doorskin glued and stapled onto the template so they touch the edge of the planking and amend the template so that it perfectly fits into the space. The amendments must not move once they are fastened to the template; strike-up marks will show if they have moved at all.

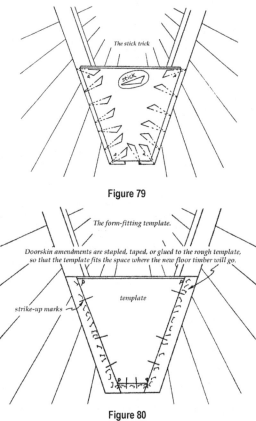

Figure 79

Figure 80

TAKING OFF BEVELS

All bevels will be taken by holding the handle of the bevel gauge along the template with the blade of the bevel gauge adjusted so it lays flat against the hull, pointing away from the frame.

When marking the bevels on the template, a distinction must be made between the two lines that define the angle by marking *inboard* on the line that represents the handle side of the bevel gauge. Take the bevels at 4- or 5-inch divisions or stations along the sides of the template. Also mark "Port" and "Starboard."

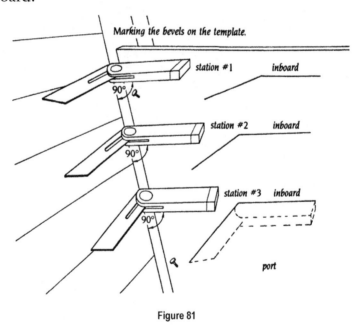

Figure 81

All the spiling marks and bevels are measured from the *inboard side* of the template, so the bevels will be transferred to the *inboard side* on the new floor timber. The new floor timber will be cut out with the *inboard side* facing up. We are measuring and cutting everything from the *inboard side.* The template was marked on its *outboard side* so it is necessary to reverse the template by transferring the spiling marks to the *inboard side* of the template .

The spiling marks are drilled through with a small drill bit in an electric drill held square to the template or a small nail may be hammered through the template to make a nail hole appear on the other side. On this reverse side the words *inboard side* are written. If the template is not reversed, then when it is cut out the floor timber will be backwards. *This error is easily avoided by simply reversing the template.*

Reversing the Divider Method Template

The spiling marks are drilled through or a small nail is driven through to transfer the marks to the reverse side of the template. The words *inboard side* are written on this reversed side of the template. The SET of the dividers is also transferred to this side.

Reversing the Stick Trick Template

Drill holes or drive small nails through the four points that define the handle of the stick. Then the four points are joined with a straight edge and pencil on the reverse side of the template and *inboard side* is marked on that side. (Figure 82)

Reversing the Form-Fitting Template

The template is flipped over to the other side and the words *inboard side* are written on it.

225

Figure 82
Drill a hole, or drive a nail through the four points to transfer the shape of the stick's handle onto the other side of the template.

TRANSFERRING THE SPILING MARKS TO THE NEW FLOOR TIMBER

It is not necessary to transfer the bevels to the reverse or *inboard side* of the template. When a suitable piece of wood has been found for the new floor timber, it should be turned so that the side you want to face *inboard* is facing up. (The crown of the grain should be facing away from the frames.) The template is nailed to the piece of wood so that the *inboard side* of the template also faces up. The spiling marks are transferred onto the new floor timber the exact way that they were taken off the hull. The SET must be checked if using dividers. The same block held the same way must be made to follow the line on the template, while the new floor timber is marked. The same stick is used to mark the points on the cutting line of the new floor timber. And the form-fitting template is simply traced onto the new floor timber.

226

Check the marks again to make sure there were no errors made transferring the spiling marks from the template to the new floor timber. Remove the template from the new floor timber and write the words *inboard side* on that side of the new floor timber.

CUTTING OUT THE NEW FLOOR TIMBER—THE BEVEL

Flip the spiling template over to the original side or consult the paper that contains the bevels and examine the bevels. Select the bevel of the greatest angle on the starboard side of the template. A protractor may help you to determine which angle to use. *The correct bevel to choose will allow the floor timber to be cut out to its greatest dimensions.*

The bevel gauge is set to this angle. The handle of the bevel gauge must be placed along the side of the bevel that is labeled *inboard.* This is also the angle that the saw blade must be set to in order to cut out the starboard side of the floor timber.

Hold the handle of the bevel gauge on the table of the bandsaw, table saw, or circular saw and adjust the table so that the saw blade is at the greatest angle at the blade of the bevel gauge.

Now, before you cut out the floor timber, go back inside the boat and draw a rough sketch of the angle of the sides of the floor timber. Mark the *inboard side* of the floor timber (Figure 83). Mark also "Port" and "Starboard" on the sketch.

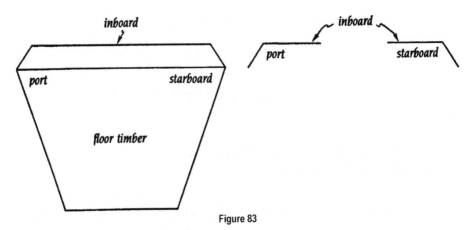

Figure 83
A rough sketch of the floor timber will show the bevel angles.

Making Floor Timbers

Now that the saw blade is set for the greatest bevel on the starboard side, place the wood for the floor timber with the *inboard side* facing up so that its starboard side is touching the blade. Now look at the rough drawing and check to make sure that the floor timber will be cut out the correct way if it is cut with the blade at this angle.

Having checked that the floor timber will be cut out at the correct bevel for the starboard side, cut out the starboard side.

Repeat the procedure for the port side and cut out the port side of the floor timber.

By cutting out the greatest angle, you have compensated for the fact that the floor timber will be wider or narrower on the *inboard side* than on the *outboard side.* Usually floor timbers are placed forward of the frames in the forward half of the boat and abaft the frames in the aft half of the boat. When the floor timbers are cut out to the greatest bevel, they thereby cut a little oversized. When the sides are planed or sanded to correspond with the bevels at each station, they can be made to fit perfectly. All that will be needed is to plane the sides down a little at each station to adjust the bevel.

Adjust the bevel of the floor timber at each station so that when the handle of the bevel gauge is pressed against the *inboard side* of the floor timber, the blade of the bevel gauge lays flat on the beveled edge of the floor timber. Adjusting the bevel is best done right up there inside the boat so that the bevel gauge can be set to the exact bevel at each station. Final fitting may be done with chalk to mark the tight spots if the floor timber will not seat all the way in against the frames.

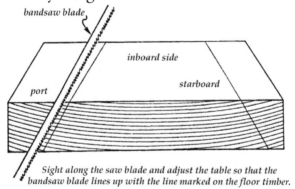

Sight along the saw blade and adjust the table so that the bandsaw blade lines up with the line marked on the floor timber.

Figure 84

FASTENING IN THE FLOOR TIMBERS

After the floor timbers fit, drill limber holes and seal in the bottom of the floor timbers with paint or epoxy. Limber holes cut in the bottom of the floor timbers facilitate adequate bilge drainage at the keel. They should be of sufficient size so they will not easily clog with bilge debris.

• *The floor timbers must be painted, especially their end grain and bottom surface.*

If the floor timber is to be drilled for a keelbolt, it should be bedded well on the bottom side and it is a good idea to make some sort of gasket between the bottom of the floor timber and the keel. Either roofing paper (tar paper), Irish felt or canvas painted with red or white lead should be used to prevent keelbolt leakage. It is also a good idea to use bedding compound of some sort between the floor timber and the frames: Dolphinite or tar. The floor timbers by way of the mast step or under the engine beds may be made thicker than the other floor timbers and there may be one floor timber at each frame in these areas even though there is only one floor timber for every other frame in other places in the boat.

Floor timbers should be fastened to the frames with three staggered carriage bolts (so the frame does not split along the grain). Rivets can also be used. The floor timber, if not through-bolted to the keel, should be drift bolted to the keel, drilling and driving the drifts in on an angle. Best not to use steel drifts.

Any places where water is trapped between floor timber and frame or below the level of the limber holes should be filled in with hot tar or epoxy. If in the engine room, where the diesel or gas and oil leaks in the bilge may cause the tar to melt or dissolve, cement or epoxy may be used.

When replacing floor timbers, the lower planks may be fastened to them in addition to the bottoms of the frames.

• *Floor timbers are very important, they tie each side of the boat together and like the deck, complete the continuity of the entire structure.*

17
SHIPWORM

The shipworm is a marine bivalve or mollusk. Basically it is a clam that lives outside its shell, a shell modified to form a drill by which it is able to bore through wood. Although there is evidence that the shipworm will eat any species of wood, some woods are more resistant than others to this destructive marine borer. Fir, oak, Philippine mahogany, and white pine are especially susceptible, while woods such as purple heart, green heart, iron bark, cypress and teak are more resistant to shipworm damage. If you can, use cypress for planking, it is the most worm resistant of these woods. Once penetration of the wood occurs, the bivalve turns at right angles and bores through the wood along the grain coating its hole with a hard, calcium-like coating. The shipworm can grow to 12 inches in length and once inside the wood, will never leave.

Long ago, boats were covered with a mixture of lime and tallow to discourage shipworm attack, and then sheathed with a sacrificial layer of green heart or iron bark. Later, vessels were sheathed with Irish felt (a kind of tar paper made of flax), horsehair, hemp, and Stockholm tar, over which copper sheathing was nailed with copper tacks. The seams of the copper plates were soldered and solder was placed over the nail heads. This method was quite effective, until it was discovered that a paint containing high percentages of cuprous oxide and other chemicals such as arsenic and mercury would protect wood from infestation of the dreaded shipworm. This paint has become less effective as harmful chemicals are banned and the antifouling paint loses its effectiveness and must be renewed annually. In areas of warmer water temperatures worm damage can be very severe, and boats must be hauled and painted more often.

In some warm water areas there are other marine borers which enter wooden boats through the seams. In Florida these are called puttybugs since they eat the soft putty in the seams of wooden-planked boats. Puttybugs look like tiny armadillos. Puttybugs can eat polyurethane, polysulphide, and pastes that are sold as "under-water seam compound." It is for this reason that soft seam compounds should not be used. Use epoxy-catalyzed lead (Splash Zone Compound), Portland cement and bottom paint mixtures for underwater seam compounds. Brackish or semi-brackish water and water with a lot of nutrients (organic pollutants) seem to attract larger populations of this marine borer than do areas of clear, clean ocean water.

When surveying for worm damage, inspect the hull for tiny holes. These holes are sometimes ⅛ inch or smaller. Examine the plank seams, and if wet, reef them out. Inspect both top and bottom seam edges for worm holes. Worms can also enter around through-hulls, between the rudder and deadwood, on the bottom and top edges of rudders, under transducers, before and abaft ballast keels, and in the seams between the ballast keel and the deadwood. Worm damage will occur especially close to the waterline at areas where antifouling paint has been scraped off due to chafe or collision with submerged or floating objects when underway or where bottom paint has been removed by straps of a travel lift.

When repairing worm damage, it is first necessary to determine the extent of the penetration of the shipworm. Stick a small wire into the hole to determine its depth. If very shallow and superficial, it will suffice to burn out the hole with a propane or butane torch and seal it up with cement or epoxy. *However, if extensive, the best way is to remove the infected wood, replace it with new wood,* and paint well with a good grade of antifouling paint. If damage is confined to a small, shallow area, inlay a diamond graving block if the planking is 1 1/4-inch thick or greater. If in deadwood, routed out to a depth that will remove all traces of worm and worm hole.

A spline or graving block should be glued over the hole that was left after removal of *ALL* the infested wood and the seam caulked with cotton, as before.

It is a good idea to copper sheathe the leading edge of the rudder and behind the sternpost because it is difficult to paint this area adequately with bottom paint. Very often, marine borers are found in this space between the rudder and the hull and the copper sheathing should keep them away.

WORMSHOE

Another particularly vulnerable place on a sailboat is the deadwood area before and abaft the ballast keel on a sailboat. It is customary that these areas be capped by a wormshoe. This is sacrificial; that is to say, that once infested by shipworm or damaged by grounding, the wormshoe can be removed and replaced to prevent the worm from penetrating the rest of the deadwood, deadwood seams, or keel. Part of the deadwood often gets neglected when bottom-painting and bare wood is often exposed as a result of going aground. If there is no wormshoe in either the deadwood before or abaft the ballast keel, it is a good idea to install one. The boat should be blocked in such a way as to allow the removal of the keel blocks under the keel at the areas where a shoe is to be replaced or installed. By setting the vessel on short keel blocks with wedges driven on top, the wedges and blocks can be removed to gain access.

In an internally-ballasted sailboat or a motor vessel, the entire bottom of the wooden keel should be capped with a wormshoe to protect it from grounding and from worm damage. The vessel will need to be jacked up by means of hydraulic jacks and the wormshoe replaced or installed in sections with generous overlapping locking scarfs. First however, all keel-bolts, deadwood bolts, or drifts that will be covered up by the wormshoe must be examined and replaced if deteriorated.

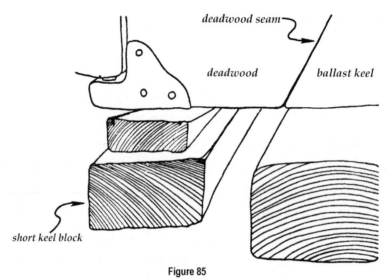

Figure 85

Use short keel blocks with wooden wedges driven above them, so that removal is possible when repairing or installing a new wormshoe

If installing a new wormshoe abaft a ballast keel, the bottom edge of the deadwood will need to be raised to the level of the top edge of the shoe to allow the bottom of the wormshoe to be on the same level as the bottom of the keel. Check to see if the ends of the keelbolts, drifts or deadwood bolts are countersunk deep enough so as not to interfere with the placement of the new wormshoe. If not, the shoe will need to be countersunk by way of these fasteners, or the fasteners shortened and countersunk to clear the upper surface of the wormshoe. Any bolts or fasteners in the deadwood will need to be marked so they can be avoided when fastening the wormshoe.

Make the wormshoe out of a hard worm-resistant wood. On the Pacific coast of the United States, the wormshoes are made out of hard wood – iron bark, purple heart, green heart.

On the Atlantic coast the general practice is to make them out of oak, fir, or pine as it is argued that they are sacrificial anyhow. However, it is my recommendation to use a worm-resistant wood for the wormshoe.

• *There is nothing wrong with making the wormshoe (or rub-rail) out of TREX, the plastic wood used for outdoor house decking.*

Make a template by tracing the shape of the bottom of the deadwood onto a piece of plywood so that the new wormshoe will fit the shape of the deadwood. Record the angle of the deadwood and keel seam with a bevel gauge. Then cut the template trace it onto a suitable piece of wood *with the crown of the wood facing downward.*

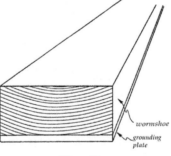

wormshoe
grounding plate

Figure 86

Where a long wormshoe needs to be joined in several sections, use one of the joints or scarfs shown here (Figure 87):

A step scarf is best on the wormshoe. These scarfs can also be used if repairing deadwood, keel timbers, or stems. Nibbed ends on scarfs should be about 25-percent of the depth of the timber and the length of the scarf should be at least six or seven times the scarf depth.

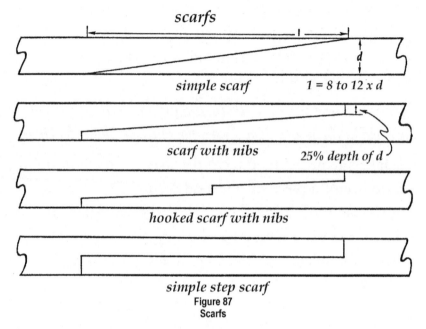

scarfs

simple scarf $1 = 8$ to 12 x d

scarf with nibs   25% depth of d

hooked scarf with nibs

simple step scarf

Figure 87
Scarfs

To prevent splitting the timbers being bolted, stagger the bolt holes through the scarfs so that they are not all along the same grain line. The distance between the center of the bolt hole and the end of the timber should be at least seven times the bolt diameter for softwoods and five times the bolt diameter for hardwoods.

• *Drill ⅜-inch holes in both surfaces scattered randomly to a depth of about ½-inch when gluing two timbers together. These "pecker holes" will trap glue in the joints when clamped and produce anti-shear locks in the joint.*

When the wormshoe is completed, drill or countersunk holes of sufficient size to allow large, flat washers under the heads of the lag bolts that will fasten the wormshoe to the deadwood. Lag bolts are generally used to fasten the wormshoe so that they can be easily removed for subsequent replacement of the wormshoe. The countersunk hole for the lag bolt and washer should be of sufficient depth to allow a wood plug to be glued over it or the countersunk hole can be filled with epoxy putty to protect the fastener.

Number 316 stainless-steel lag bolts or silicone bronze should be ⅜ inch or larger and their length at least twice the thickness of the wormshoe. If bronze lag bolts are used, they should be of a greater diameter than they would be if using a harder metal.

After the holes are drilled in the wormshoe, it is a good idea to paint it with several coats of bottom paint as it will be more difficult to do this after the wormshoe is installed. Seal especially the end grain and around the countersunk holes with bottom paint. Make a gasket cut out of heavy grade roofing tar paper or Irish felt to fit between the wormshoe and the deadwood or keel. A thick mixture of plastic roofing tar (you can buy water-proof roofing cement, a tar-like mixture for repairing and bedding flashing on roofs at a lumberyard or hardware store) mixed with antifouling paint forms an excellent bedding compound between the deadwood the roofing paper gasket and the upper surface of the wormshoe.

Align the wormshoe up against the gasket, replace the keel blocks, drive wooden wedges between the block and the wormshoe. Use a hydraulic jack to tighten the wormshoe against the deadwood or keel. Then drill the holes into the deadwood, using the holes pre-drilled in the wormshoe as drilling guides. If the space between the wormshoe and the ground is too small to use an electric drill with a 90° angle drive in its chuck, then drive the lag bolts halfway into the deadwood with a heavy sledge hammer, and tightened the rest of the way with a ratchet and socket. It is also a good idea to fasten a metal plate on the bottom surface of the wormshoe to protect it from grounding damage.

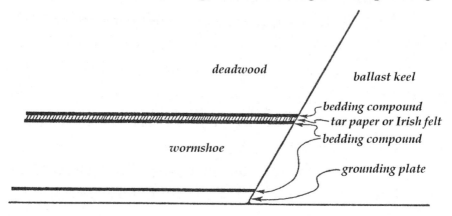

Figure 88

18

STEMS

SURVEYING THE STEM

Examine the stem head, especially under the bowsprit, for rotten wood caused by fresh water entering along the exposed end grain at the top of the stem. Look for crushed wood fibers at or below the waterline that may indicate collision or grounding. Examine the bolts for leaking or deterioration and the adjacent wood around the bolt holes for soundness. Check at the bobstay for electrolysis-softened wood. As metals corrode, chemicals are produced which soften the surrounding wood. Look for bubbles in paint indicating the wood beneath is wet. Check the inboard side of the stem and at the bottom of the chain locker where fresh water entering through an anchor chain deck pipe may collect and rot the stem or stem knee from the inside. Inspect the breasthook and apron and any places that may trap water between frame and stem. Look for poor ventilation that promotes fungus and bacterial growth that will cause rot. Hammer on the stem. Listen for the dull sound of soft wood.

REPAIRING THE STEM

If you find deteriorated wood at the stem head or around the bobstay fitting, it should be carefully inspected to determine the extent of the deterioration. If the damage is confined to a small area and does not structurally weaken the entire timber, it will suffice to replace only the deteriorated wood in that area. Make a cap to replace a damaged stem head or a graving block to repair a section of wood damaged by corrosion, collision, or grounding.

Structural graving block.

cap the top to prevent water from entering stem head at end grain

breasthook

bolted through apron and breasthook

cutwater

structural graving block

apron

bolted through apron

original stem

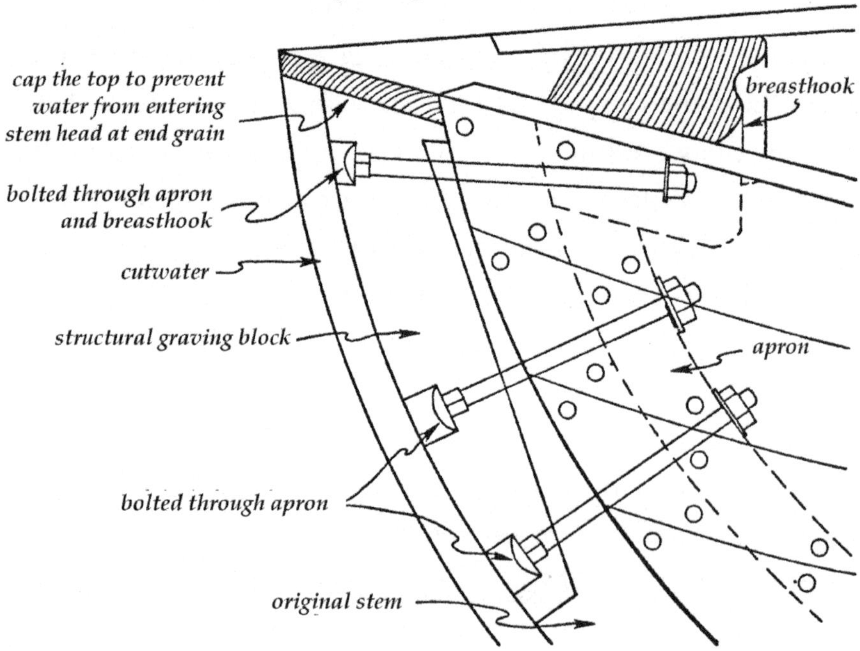

Figure 89

The entire leading edge of the stem can be cut and planed back to good wood and a new tapered outboard leading edge can be added. This is called a "cutwater" and usually caps over the bolts that secure the stem scarfs together or that bolt the stem to the apron or knee. If a graving block is added to the stem where a bobstay fitting corroded or damaged the wood, it will be wise to relocate and redesign the fitting after repairing the damage caused by the original one. When fastening a graving block, have the grain run in the same direction as the grain in the adjacent wood. The wood grain should run nearly at right angles to the fasteners. Structural graving pieces should have adequate dimensions and well-proportioned, glued, and through-bolted scarf joints. Non-structural graving blocks that replace superficial damage should be glued into the timber they repair.

Remember that the bowsprit should nearly bisect the angle between the bobstay and the headstay and should be raised above the deck. If moving the bobstay fitting will decrease the angle and weaken the resistance to the upward thrust of the headstay load, it may be necessary to install a dolphin striker along the bobstay.

When the damaged part is forward of the rabbet, the outboard part of the stem can be cut back to inside the rabbet and the planks can be left fastened to the remaining part of the original stem. The new outboard stem can be glued and bolted through the remaining stem and a large apron added inboard of the original stem through which all the parts are bolted. This type of construction is called a "battened stem."

If unable to steam bend or locate the appropriate wood for sawing out the new curved stem, one may be laminated out of individually glued and fastened layers. When using large timbers to rebuild stem or backbone assemblies, always drill pecker holes in both surfaces prior to gluing. The timbers can even be pre-soaked in salt water and steamed before use.

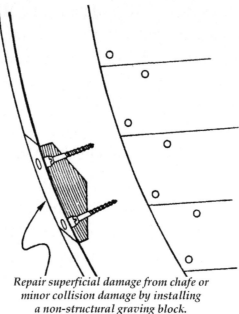

Repair superficial damage from chafe or minor collision damage by installing a non-structural graving block.

Figure 90

REPLACING THE STEM

It is very important to be realistic in appraising the extent of the damage and the type of repair that is appropriate. Don't be too hasty. If a little end grain rot is found or some superficial worm damage, don't rip out the entire stem. However, if it has been decided that the entire stem needs replacing, it will be much better to unfasten the planking ends and unbolt the stem, trying to remove it in large pieces if possible so that they can be used as templates to measure for the new replacement. Examine closely the hood ends of the planks, remove the paint and check for split ends or soft, over-fastened wood at the plank ends. If it doesn't appear that these plank ends can be saved and refastened to the new stem, there are two choices: either replace these bow planks with long well-staggered lengths of new planks or, if only the very ends of the planks are bad, you may decide to cut back these planks an inch or two to where they are solid again and redesign the stem so that the new stem will be thicker at the rabbet and extend back far enough to accommodate fastening of the cut-back plank ends.

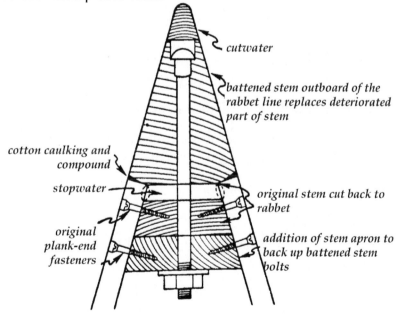

Figure 91

Sometimes when replacing a stem, the planks on one side can be removed and the ones on the other side left and the end fasteners backed out to mark where the rabbet of the new stem goes and aid in fitting the sections of the new stem.

The addition of an apron is very useful when replacing the stem. The planks should be fastened to the apron as well as to the stem rabbet. Place stopwaters along the rabbet where any scarf or joint passes through the rabbet before fastening the planks to the stem.

If it is necessary to replace the planks at the bow as well as replacing the stem, leave every other plank or as many as possible to allow removal of the original stem and fitting of the new stem. This way the location of the rabbet can be determined and marked on the new stem.

When replacing a stem or stem assembly, it is helpful to make full-size templates out of scrap pieces of fir or pine to discover if there are any hidden problems that you will run into when cutting and fitting the new timber.

When selecting wood for stem or stern assemblies, choose wood that has grain similar to the shape of the timber being replaced.

• *When epoxying two big pieces of wood together, drill "pecker holes" — ⅜-inch holes about ½-inch deep randomly in both surfaces to trap glue and make an anti-shear bond. Making tight Japanese carpentry smooth joints in timbers will not allow enough glue to adequately join the two pieces when they are clamped.*

When fastening knees, angle the bolts so that their angle actually pulls the knee tighter into the joint. This angle is not usually a 90° angle. Use shores and wedges, hydraulic jacks, and come-alongs to force structural timbers tightly together before fastening.

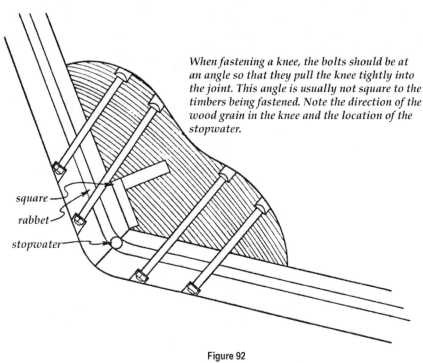

When fastening a knee, the bolts should be at an angle so that they pull the knee tightly into the joint. This angle is usually not square to the timbers being fastened. Note the direction of the wood grain in the knee and the location of the stopwater.

square

rabbet

stopwater

Figure 92

Stopwaters

Stopwaters are the only places where a dowel with exposed end grain is used on a wooden boat Stopwaters are driven into a hole drilled right through a joint that crosses the rabbet line in the deadwood, stem, keel, or stern post assemblies. The stopwater should extend through the timber from one side of the boat to the other. They are usually the same size or a bit smaller in diameter than the thickness of the planking and are made out of a soft wood such as cedar, cypress, or redwood. They are whittled out with a knife and driven tight and dry into the hole. Cut the stopwater off flush with a saw; sand and paint the end grain with bottom paint. When the stopwater swells, it tightens in its hole and stops the water from following the joint or seam into the boat. There should be one or two stopwaters, if possible, under the planking along every scarf that intersects the rabbet line.

19

THROUGH-HULL VALVES

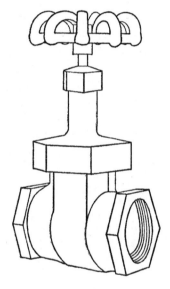

Figure 93
Gate Valve

• *This is a gate valve* (Figure 93). It has no business being on your boat. If your boat is hauled out, this is a good time to remove and replace it. This type of valve has a brass stem and a steel handle. It will corrode very quickly. Also, it cannot be serviced. Replace it with a good ball valve–not a plastic one.

249

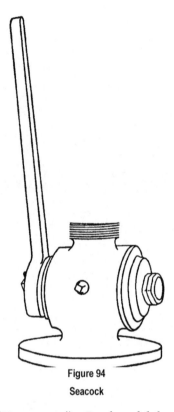

Figure 94
Seacock

• *This is a seacock* (Figure 94). It should be inspected and serviced every year when your boat is hauled out. These fittings were common up to the '80s after that, ball valves were used. It is advised to replace these fittings with new ball valves.

Remove the two lock nuts that hold the tapered barrel in the casting, remove the large end washer, and remember or draw a diagram of how it fits on the end. Turn the handle if you can and or tap gently with a piece of wood or rubber mallet on the threaded part where the two lock nuts were and remove the tapered barrel from the casting. Be careful not to damage the threads; you may want to back the nuts a bit but leave the nuts on them while tapping on the end to protect these threads. Inspect the tapered barrel for corrosion and grooves in its surface.

Rotate the barrel against fine emery paper or 400-grit wet-and-dry sand paper and rubbing compound. Replace the tapered barrel in the body of the casting and rotate it back and forth to clean and fit the two surfaces together. Do this until the barrel is smooth. Wipe all the rubbing compound off with alcohol or mineral spirits. Check the inside of the casting with your finger for roughness or corrosion, and if necessary, insert a piece of wet-and-dry or emery paper in the casting and smooth it out inside. If it is very badly scored, the seacock may need to be replaced. Be sure to remove all rubbing compound or it will damage the surfaces when you assemble them and cause the valve to jam. If you are able to get both surfaces smooth again and cleaned up, then coat all surfaces with a film of waterproof grease such as wheel bearing grease, graphite-less pump grease. *Don't use any grease containing graphite.* Reassemble the valve the same way it was before you took it apart. Adjust the lock nut so that the tapered barrel fits snugly, but not so tight that it takes undue pressure to turn the handle. If the surfaces were too corroded or scratched to smooth out by sanding with rubbing compound or it is old and you decide to replace the seacock, use a good quality modern ball valve.

BALL VALVES

Ball valves have a stainless steel ball that turns in a nylon or

251

Teflon seat. This is the best type of valve. If the through valves have never been replaced, replace them with ball valve backing plates, good reinforced Coast Guard approved hoses and good hose clamps. Double hose clamps below the waterline and within 12 inches above the waterline.

• *Every through-hull valve must have a backing block under it.*

These backing blocks are the same design as the buttblocks described in the chapter on planking. They have a beveled top edge, and are bedded well with bedding compound (either poly-sulfide, polyurethane, plastic roofing tar, or Dolphinite) and fitted to the curve of the hull. Use an expansion bit or a hole saw to cut a hole in the middle of the block. Be sure to seal the block's hole and end grain well with paint. Also carefully seal the end grain around the hole in the plank for the through-hull with paint or epoxy.

INSTALLING A NEW SEA VALVE OR TIGHTENING A SEA VALVE ON A THROUGH-HULL

Imagine you are holding a through-hull valve and tightening it (turning it clockwise). Imagine you are holding the through-hull outside the hull, and tightening it onto the valve (turning it clockwise, also). Both hands are turning in a clockwise direction that will tighten together the two objects they are holding, but both hands are turning in the opposite direction to each other. Now with your left hand only, turn the imaginary valve clockwise to tighten it. Which way will this cause the through-hull to turn? *Counterclockwise.*

So, if you try to tighten a valve from the inside of the boat without having someone on the outside holding the through-hull from turning, you will be backing out the through-hull! The harder you tighten the valve from the inside, the looser the through-hull will fit against the planking on the outside. You may not notice that you've loosened the through-hull, but you will when the boat is back in the water.

• *Never tighten a valve from the inside without having someone on the outside to stop the through-hull from turning.*

How are you going to hold the thing from turning? Look inside the through-hull fitting from the outside, you should see two little lumps or ridges. If your through-hull fitting doesn't have these bumps it is probably so old that it needs to be replaced. Replace it with one that has those two bumps inside.

• *Don't use a plastic through-hull.*

These cannot be tightened sufficiently without stripping their threads. Buy bronze through-hulls. These are the biggest holes in your boat. Be sure to install, inspect and maintain them correctly.

Ask your welder friend to cut a triangle out of ¼-inch steel plate. It should be roughly 8 inches long and 3 inches at the wide end, tapering to a point at the other end. This will be your *through-hull key.* It gets hammered point-first into the hole in the through-hull fitting until it jams up against the two bumps in the casting. Hold the outboard end of the through-hull key with a pipe wrench. Put a longer section of pipe over the handle of the pipe wrench. That's how your friend will hold the through-hull from turning while you are tightening the valve from the inside.

Sometimes there is not enough room to turn the valve from the inside, and the only way to remove it if you need to put a backing block under it or replace the valve is by unscrewing the through-hull from the outside while the valve is being held from turning by a pipe wrench and cheater pipe from the inside.

Remember to put plenty of bedding compound, Dolphinite, white lead, or wet patch under the backing block and mix some antifouling paint in with the bedding compound under the through-hull when reassembling it. Make a ring out of caulking cotton and place it under the through-hull flange. Sometimes the valve casting base has holes drilled in it and can also be secured to the backing block with screws or bolts after it is tightened on the through-hull. This reduces the possibility of the seacock breaking off at the end of the through-hull threads if someone were to step on it or if something falls on the valve.

When replacing the hose on the valve, inspect it for signs of deterioration. Never use rubber heater-type automotive hoses or garden hoses. Buy the best quality reinforced hose that is made for the purpose for which it will be used. Put all fittings together with a good joint compound or Teflon tape. *Never mix metals;* if you're using bronze pipe fittings, never use steel pipe fittings with them. Electrical tape wrapped around the hose under a hose clamp may prevent the clamp from cutting the hose. Use double stainless steel hose clamps wherever possible—the expensive kind with 316 tightening bolts. If the hose won't quite fit on the end of the hose barb, stick the end of the hose in boiling water to soften it up and make it more flexible before jamming it on the fitting. Or soften it up with a heat gun. Put grease or soap under the hose to help it slide on the fitting.

• *Don't use a close nipple under a hose, use a hose barb.*

Hang a tapered wood bung from the valve, to fit the hole that would remain after the valve accidently broke off. If you are unable to buy one this size, a wooden fid with the point cut off will suffice. There should be one tapered bung hanging on a lanyard from each through-hull on your boat.

The Coast Guard requires that all inspected vessels pull the hoses off the valves every haul inspection. This makes sense because it gives the boat owner a chance to observe if there is deterioration in the connection between the valve and the hose. Lots of times there are common brass or steel close nipple pipes threaded into the valve that corrode through instead of proper hose barbs. Also this provides for a good test and inspection of the hose and all the components of the valve. Turn all through-hull valves on and off several times a year and lubricate with WD-40 or the like to keep them operating freely. *All through-hull valves must operate freely or be replaced.*

20

COLD-MOLDING OVER AN EXISTING WOODEN BOAT

When considering how to restore a wooden boat, you may decide the boat cannot or should not be repaired using traditional methods.

One large wooden boat was fastened with copper rivets. When several of the rivets were removed for inspection after the boat was over 30 years old, the rivets were so deteriorated that they easily broke and crumbled when bent between two vise grips. This sailboat had a beautiful all solid teak interior with no access to the inboard side of the frames for replacing rivets without totally gutting the interior. In this case, the owner decided to cold-mold over the existing hull, since the hull was still structurally sound and no rot was found in the planking or deadwood.

In the process of cold-molding, the hull is allowed to dry out and new layers of wood, epoxy and fiberglass applied so that they form a structural layer.

First the paint is removed from the hull by grinding or sand-blasting. The hull dries out. Seams are splined by removing the cotton caulking and epoxying wood wedges into the seams and butts to make the surface all wood. Through-hull fittings and all hardware attachments are removed from the hull. If the boat has a ballast keel, the keel is encapsulated in heavy fiberglass matt and woven glass and the layers of cold-molding overlapped over the keel encapsulation.

A layer of about ⅜-inch x 4-inch diagonal strips of white cedar or other good boat building wood *(never plywood)* are epoxied and monel stapled to the hull. Then the process is repeated in the opposite direction at 90 degrees to the first layer, using thickened epoxy in between layers.

Several coats of epoxy-saturated fiberglass matt, woven glass and finish cloth are applied; epoxy fairing compound trowelled on, the hull faired, painted and the through-hulls and hardware replaced.

Care must be taken to epoxy and glass the deck to the cold molded hull to avoid allowing fresh water to enter anywhere between the cold-molding and the original hull.

21

DECKS

Wooden boats rot from the deck down.

Astrong, well-sealed deck is the key to keeping your wooden boat healthy. The purists love that teak, white pine, or fir-planked deck. They turn up their little noses at a plywood deck covered with fiberglass cloth and epoxy resin. I have yet to see a wooden planked deck that doesn't shrink in hot, dry season and leak in rainy season and whose surface is not too hot to walk on barefoot on a bright sunny day in the tropics.

If you insist on a planked wood deck, wood plugs must be kept well-sealed to protect the fasteners, sub-deck, deck beams and the rest of the hull from rotting. Caulked seams must be caulked perfectly with cotton, payed with paint and filled with the best black rubbery stuff money can buy. If that beautiful wood-planked deck leaks, the hull will rot from the inside out. If you insist on that single wood-plank deck, you must commit to the maintenance.

Still others purists insist that the painted canvas-covered

deck and cabintop is the way to roll.

A boat's deck must be waterproof and strong. A good strong deck completes the structure of the hull.

A non-skid painted, thick-layered, glass fiber and epoxy resin covering over good, well epoxy-saturated marine plywood makes a strong waterproof deck.

Every sailboat with a keel-stepped mast must have a water-tight mast boot to keep rainwater out of the mast step. Insert stopwaters above the mast boot angling upward on any check or crack in the mast that extends below the mastboot.

Cabin corner posts should not leak.

Stanchion bases should not leak, put them on a teak or other rot-resistant pad and bed them well and install a butt under the deck for through bolting. Cabin tops should not leak, they should be covered with a good waterproof covering and well painted. Wood trim around the upper and/or lower edge of the cabin needs to be well-bedded and well-fastened or removed to stop leaks. Hatches and companionways should not leak; they need to be re-designed and any rot around them repaired.

• *Never hose down the deck of a wood boat with fresh water.*

• *Use salt water to clean the deck of your wood boat. And bucket off the deck with salt water after it rains. Salt water will help stop your boat from rotting from the inside out.*

22

RIGGING THE WOODEN SCHOONER OR TRADITIONAL WOODEN CRUISING SAILBOAT

So much has been forgotten about wooden boats—the old ways are gone—but the old boats are still here. In the old days nobody would ever rig a wooden boat's shrouds with anything else but deadeyes and lanyards. Turnbuckles on a steel boat, on a fiberglass boat, on an aluminum boat. But *not* on a wooden boat (except for a very few wooden racing yachts which were never expected to last very long). (Figures 95 and 96)

The traditional wooden boat and especially the schooner rig was designed to be low stress, hand tight—not bar tight—stout masts keel stepped through heavy mast partners with deadeyes and lanyards as shock absorbers to resist transferring dynamic loads to the hull. The rigging does not hold up the mast; it is only there to steady the mast. Deadeyes and lanyards save the hull and masts from tremendous rig loads. A wooden mast should not be rigged so it is too rigid; it has to bend and give. Wood's strength is in its flexibility.

Figure 95
Close-up of Lower Deadeye

Figure 96
Deadeyes and Lanyards

Turnbuckles on a wooden boat cause too much internal compression of the mast and transmit the loads to the hull where they can deform (hog) the sheer of a hull, break frames below the chain plates, separate hull planks, lift decks, loosen the garboards, break masts and in some cases drive the mast through the keel.

Spreaders should bisect the angle at the shrouds and their outboard ends should be well-secured to the shrouds to prevent slipping. Parceling and serving the shrouds at the spreaders makes it easier to secure the spreader ends to the shrouds.

When replacing spreaders, use rot-resistant teak or ipe, not spruce, not oak or fir.

WATERPROOF COATINGS FOR A WOODEN MAST

A great coating for a wooden mast is a home-made paste wax mixture of beeswax and corn oil. Both have fungicidal properties. Melt the beeswax in a coffee can and add corn oil—the mixture is about one-part beeswax, three or four parts corn oil—to make a paste wax of the desired consistency when cooled. Rub this mixture after it cools on the wooden masts with a rag from a bosun's chair whenever the masts look dry. The wood will not turn gray or black but remains bright, colorful, and waterproof. Rub the beeswax mixture into the cracks and checks to seal them and to keep out rainwater and wood-boring insects. Use the mixture on any bare wood surface.

Varnish on masts may last a bit longer and look pretty for a while. But varnish requires a lot of maintenance, sanding, re-applying and removing when it finally gives up and the time comes to renew it. Varnish will crack from the sun, and from halyards and mast hoops scratching and slapping on the mast; then fresh water gets beneath to rot the wood.

Linseed oil promotes fungal growth and Vaseline, a petroleum product, dissolves the lignum, the natural glue that holds the wood fibers together. The popular treatment for solid wood masts, a combination of linseed oil and Vaseline, promotes mast rot. And don't leave the checks open to breathe, they will breathe fresh water which will cause them to rot. Open checks and cracks in masts will also attract wood-boring insects (termites, carpenter bees, carpenter ants). Instead, fill all the checks and cracks with your thickened mixture of beeswax and corn oil or polysulphide.

Use good American-made galvanized shackles when rigging. Stainless steel and cheap Chinese shackles won't last long.

SQUARE RIGGERS' ROUND SEIZINGS — DEAD EYES

Parcel and service 7 x 19 #316 stainless steel rigging wire for shrouds. Use friction tape (old-fashioned tar-covered cloth tape) to cover the wire in the same direction as the lay of the wire. Then wrap over the friction tape tightly with tarred marlin, (tarred nylon) wrapping the opposite direction. Cover the seizing and serving with Stockholm tar, pine tar or your mixture of beeswax and corn oil. Turn the serviced wire around a deadeye and make four round seizings. This is better than using nicropress and stay-lock fittings. Rove the lanyard through the deadeye with the stopper knot (Mathew Walker knot) facing inboard through the upper right hole in the upper deadeye. Adjust the port deadeyes hand-tight when on a starboard tack, the starboard deadeyes hand-tight when on a port tack. (Figures 97 and 98)

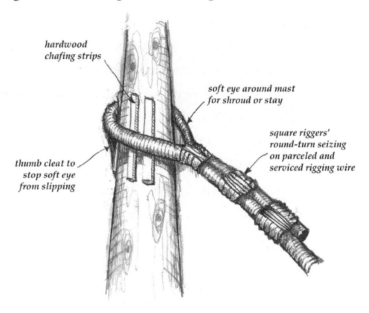

hardwood chafing strips

soft eye around mast for shroud or stay

square riggers' round-turn seizing on parceled and serviced rigging wire

thumb cleat to stop soft eye from slipping

Figure 97
Soft eye around mast to secure rigging wire to mast

SQUARE RIGGERS' ROUND SEIZINGS — SOFT EYES

When attaching shrouds and stays to the mast, soft eyes made of parceled and serviced 7 x 19 rigging wire with four or more round turns of a square rigger's seizing is more dependable than relying on metal mast bands and mast tangs. I have never seen a soft eye with a square rigger's seizing fail, but I've seen stay-locks and nicropresses and metal mast bands and tangs slip, break and fail. (Figures 97, 98 and 99)

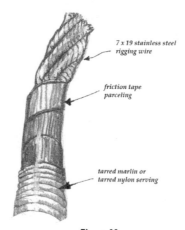

*7 x 19 stainless steel
rigging wire*

*friction tape
parceling*

*tarred marlin or
tarred nylon serving*

Figure 98
Parceled and serviced #316 stainless steel 7 x 19 rigging wire

Figure 99
Upper Deadeye showing square riggers' four round seizings

265

REPAIRING BROKEN SPARS

When repairing a broken mast or spar, build a simple scarfing jig out of plywood or planks and screw aluminum strips to the two upper surfaces as a guide for sawing and planning. (Figure 100)

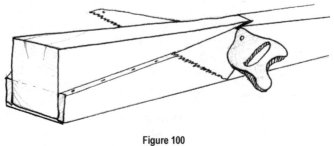

Figure 100
Scarfing jig

Use the jig to cut scarf angles in the mast or spar and in the wood chosen for repair. Make a "clothes pin" scarf. (Figure 101)

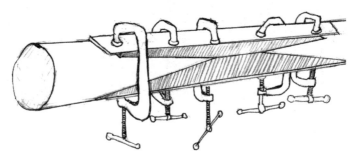

Figure 101
Clothes pin scarf

Drill "pecker holes" or ⅜-inch holes in the surfaces of all joints before applying epoxy and clamping to trap glue in the joints and make them anti-shear and self-locking.

To reduce the diameter of a round timber, turn it into a square, then turn the square into an eight-sided shape and round as desired.

BULL DOG CLAMPS OR CABLE CLAMPS —NEVER SADDLE A DEAD HORSE

Found on cable steering where the 7 x 19 cable attaches to the steering quadrant. Cable clamps are used so that cables can be adjusted after they stretch.

Also used for emergency repairs to standing rigging, on centerboard cables, travel lifts, fork lifts, cranes, on roller-coasters and other scary carnival rides.

If the saddle is installed on the dead-end side of the cable, it will squash and flatten the cable and the dead-end could then, under load, slide through the clamp. That's when the crane drops its load, the rudder disconnects, centerboard falls, or the roller coaster crashes.

Always install the saddle on the standing side of the cable.
Never on the dead-end side.

Easy way to remember by learning this old-school saying: **"NEVER SADDLE A DEAD HORSE"**. You will be shocked how many times cable clamps are used incorrectly.

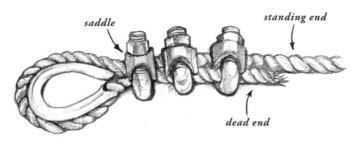

saddle   *standing end*

dead end

Figure 102

EPILOGUE

Some people make a mess when they work and clean up only once at the end of the job when the work is done. Others can't tolerate a mess at any time and need to constantly stop work to clean up and put everything back in its place.

Working on boats is like going to war. It is impossible to do it without making a mess. The bigger the job, the bigger the mess. Cleaning and organization are essential and improve the quality of your work.

Some people will not do anything unless they are sure that it will turn out perfectly, even if it means watching their boat disintegrate until they are sure that they are able to do a perfect job.

Others will make temporary repairs to prevent the situation from becoming worse.

Still others develop the symptoms of the weakness of their boats. If the boat has broken frames, they may walk around holding their ribs, and when their boat is fixed they are magically cured and feel great. It is true that there are few more wonderful, therapeutic, and satisfying feelings than fixing your own boat. The more together his boat is, the better the boat owner feels about himself.

We all secretly want our boats to be perfect and it is with great emotional anxiety and frustration that we face the reality that they may not be. Our boats are so much an extension of ourselves, our emotion, our perfection, our love, and our dreams that it is difficult to regard them with the objectivity that is necessary to drive the hammer, claw-first, into the source of their imperfection.

Others are so closely connected to their boat that it will "tell" them when something is wrong or needs attention or to be fixed. These Zen boat owners are somehow able, with a minimum amount of effort, to keep their boats in excellent condition. They are able to notice and take care of a situation before it becomes a serious problem.

For most boat owners, working on their own boats is one of the hardest physical and emotional things they will ever do. Some will never be able to work on their own boats and will need to hire others to do the work for them. Everyone has his own way of doing things; all I can tell you is that when it comes to taking care of your boat, you have to do it any way you can.

Nobody every really owns a boat, just as nobody ever really owns a horse, a bird, a tree, or a sunset. We pay for our turn to take care of and use the boat.

Hopefully your wooden boat will give you pleasure. Hopefully your wooden boat will be strong and brave and safe and take you to amazing places and adventures, last a lifetime and continue to live on after you are gone. A boat is a dream made real. With ownership comes the responsibility to keep the boat and that dream alive.

In ancient China there is a proverb, roughly translated it says: *a good master is well served...*

LONG LIVE THE WOOD BOAT!

ABOUT THE AUTHOR

Allen (Capt. Al) Cody Taube is a NAMS Global Marine Surveyor and well known boat specialist. He is a graduate architect from the Rhode Island School of Design, a licensed 100-Ton Captain, and an independent shipwright. He has owned, restored and sailed his own wooden schooners and others for 45 years. His wide-ranging experience includes building traditional sailboats and rebuilding large sailing craft, mostly schooners, including his current home, a traditional cruising wooden schooner built out of tide water cypress and Monel nails in 1972.

His first book on wooden boat repair, *The Boatwright's Companion,* published in 1986, has become the wooden boat owners' bible. "The Art of Wooden Boat Repair: How to save wood boats" is an updated, enlarged edition of the first book and is destined to become a wooden boat owner's and wooden boat lover's favorite classic book.

Allen writes feature articles for WoodenBoat Magazine and Southwinds Magazine. He has sailed extensively on the Pacific, Atlantic, North Sea and Baltic. He has worked as a commercial salvage diver, commercial fisherman and worked tugs in British Columbia. Mr. Taube is also an award-winning screenwriter and artist. He has salt water in his veins and currently lives aboard his 65 foot wooden schooner *Reef Chief* in Key West, Florida, and the Bahamas.

Index

trunnels 217

Printed in Great Britain
by Amazon

42099871R00163